REVOLUTIONARY CONVERSATIONS™

A S.H.A.R.E.™ BOOK

REVOLUTIONARY CONVERSATIONS™

A S.H.A.R.E.™ BOOK

The Tools You Need for the Success You Want

Mark H. Fowler
Noal McDonald
Barbara Gaughen-Muller

REVOLUTIONARY CONVERSATIONS, LLC

Edited by Toni Sciarra Poynter
Designed by Lorie Pagnozzi
Cover design by Georgia Morrissey
Cover art © Shutterstock

ISBN: 978-0-9911468-2-6

TO GLORIA AXELROD GOFORTH

CHERISHED FRIEND, EXCEPTIONAL MENTOR

....

"Life is a matter of dealing with other people,
in little matters and cataclysmic ones,
and that means a series of conversations."

—DEBORAH TANNEN

CONTENTS

CHAPTER 3: HELP—The Word that Empowers Us All   41

CHAPTER 4: ASK—The Key to Understanding   59

CHAPTER 5: RISK—Opening Doors to Infinite Possibilities   87

CHAPTER 7: Create Your Own Revolutionary Conversations™ with the S.H.A.R.E.™ Tools   151

AUTHORS' PREFACES
IT'S THE PEOPLE

AFTER YEARS OF WORKING WITH COMPLEX SITUATIONS, the one thing that stands out is how many people want to—and do—step forward to do the right thing. I know of so many team members in the businesses we've worked with that have led with their hearts and minds to make a difference, a big difference.

I was so impressed with this realization early in my career that I decided that being a better communicator (I was no star here) was essential for my own development. I also realized that my desire to increase the effectiveness and efficiency of our reengineering projects depended on everyone being on the same page. I took classes at UCLA Extension to learn how to be better at interacting with others. There, I met my to-be partner, Gloria Axelrod. She ran an Active Listening program for the Extension and was part of the teaching the teachers program. We ended up working together on developing clients and teaching classes.

While watching student role plays in our workshops, I discovered that there were certain actions, pieces of a conversation, that students instinctually did that helped facilitate conversation. Some of what they did was influenced by our work, but mostly it appeared to be things that they learned intuitively or from others. This is where the S.H.A.R.E.™ Tools got their start. It took several years to put these together and understand how they could work interactively to advance conversation to another level, becoming the Tools we have today.

This is definitely a road-tested program. It was important that the Tools be natural, not contrived, honest, as simple as possible, and something that brought forth true collaboration and a genuine approach to conversation.

Today, the power of these simple approaches never ceases to amaze us. There are almost "pinch me" moments that make us realize how easy it can be to embrace change, move through challenge, and build a bridge with others to more opportunity and less confusion.

Experience has taught me that STOP is my most important prevention Tool. HELP gets me to a place where I see others as friends, not people trying to ruin my project. ASK helps me realize that I need to fill in the blanks and help build a picture of what we can really do together so I/we can take a RISK to have a bigger future together. Once we roll up our sleeves, we can EXPLORE a new level of solutions never available on our own.

This might sound like a sales pitch, but it's not. It's so important to have others in our lives who support us and whom we support in turn. We are not alone and we clearly need others. I feel so blessed that I have two wonderful partners, Noal and Barbara, who help me, and we all help each other maintain and enhance our interactive skills.

The Tools have worked exceedingly well with client projects and have helped me to be much better day to day with others. We believe that there are many situations in life that could be much better—more effective, more friendly, honest, loving, and successful—and the Tools can add so much to making this a reality. We are committed to using these little powerhouses in our own disciplines and introducing them to the world.

As mentioned, what stands out for me after years of dealing with complicated and challenging situations is that deep down, most people want to do the right thing. When given a way to interact without blame and judgment, people embrace the opportunity to be better, do better, and be part of the solution, not the problem. We'd like to see that be the status quo, replacing the win/lose, my idea/your idea face-offs that we're often confronted with daily. We hope you do, too.

THE S.H.A.R.E.™ TOOLS AT WORK

NOAL MCDONALD

MARK AND I MET A NUMBER OF YEARS AGO. We found that we had many core values in common, especially the need to respect and collaborate with everyone in an organization. We had the opportunity to work together with clients, and Mark began to teach me the S.H.A.R.E.™ Tools. The more we worked together using the Tools with clients, the more it became apparent that the time had come to take this powerful conversation technology to a much broader audience.

We gathered our core group—Mark, a turnaround expert; Barbara, a high-powered PR agent; and me, a human resources (HR) professional—to talk about how to make this book a reality. We were held together through thick and thin (and believe me, there were some thin times) by our individual and collective passion about the power of conversation. What came along several years later is the book you hold in your hands and an abiding bond between the three of us.

You'll read about how the Tools help Mark and his clients turn businesses around and increase their success. Barbara shares in her preface her view of how the Tools can lead us toward world peace. I saw more and more ways the Tools could support my colleagues in human resources. Our discipline is focused entirely on people: developing employees to their full potential in the workplace, building effective teams, delivering difficult messages with respect and clarity, and maximizing the potential of the individual and the organization for everyone's benefit. And dealing with people is pretty much all about conversations.

As I write this preface, there are three challenges waiting for me at work next week. I expect these or similar ones may be on your agenda, too, since they are issues we face in business all the time.

There's a supervisor at our office who has years of experience but who is struggling with changes that have been made in the company's organizational structure and reporting processes. He's a valued employee, but he's spinning his wheels. I can see that every day is taking a toll on him. I know I can use the Tools to start a conversation with him that is nonthreatening and that will, I hope, prove productive for both of us. The gentleness of HELP and the inclusiveness of collaborative questions in ASK will help me engage him in discovering the barriers that are preventing him from connecting and being as successful as I know he can be.

The new structure has also created a very diverse group of middle managers who have come from different divisions in the company. As we bring them together, we need to find a way to create a strong, effective team. There are lots of team-building activities that we can use, but the foundation will be the S.H.A.R.E.™ Tools. Even with just the basics, they'll have a way to talk with each other that is grounded in collaboration, not confrontation or power plays. We'll be able to get the group up and running together quickly because they'll have a common language to deal with issues as they come up.

At a strategic level, our HR department is charged with designing and implementing an organization-wide continuing education program. While everyone supports it in theory, in reality department heads are less inclined to participate when it means pulling their staff away from projects to attend or teach course work. It is essential to implement this program if we want to remain competitive in the market. I'll need all the Tools I have at my disposal to create a collaborative environment to bring this project to completion.

In these and in every situation, conversation is the energy source—the connection—for all of us that focuses and releases our knowledge, creativity, and innovation. For the first time, we have a way to fully liberate that energy with the S.H.A.R.E.™ Tools. They are an essential part of my work. And I fervently hope and believe that *Revolutionary Conversations*™ and the S.H.A.R.E.™ Tools will become HR's most powerful asset in the ever-changing world of people and business.

PEACE AND HARMONY

BARBARA GAUGHEN-MULLER

I'M THE DREAMER OF THE TRIO. My daily thoughts are for peace and harmony among nations and in families, where every child will be safe and live happily. In the mid-1990s I met, fell in love with, and married Dr. Robert Muller, former United Nations Assistant Secretary-General, at a La Casa de Maria Invitational for world leaders. Together we traveled the globe, speaking about and spreading the ideas outlined in our book, *7500 Ideas and Dreams for a Better World.* In every country we visited, we found proof that we all had the same dreams for a better world, one where we live in harmony with each other and with nature. Why was this dream so impossible?

Collaborating with Mark and Noal for the past three years has helped me uncover the answer. What if the solution to conflict, tension, and war was in the conversations that preceded them? I observed the S.H.A.R.E.™ Tools being taught and practiced in our seminars and used them with businesses, NGOs, and nonprofit organizations. The results showed that we can indeed have Revolutionary Conversations™ using the S.H.A.R.E.™ Tools. Their simple steps unleashed the potential for transformational change where we came together in harmony and understanding with results that could change history.

In my board meetings as president of the Santa Barbara and Tri-County chapter of the United Nations Association of the United States of America (UNA-USA), we say, "*Palabras* first." It's an African adage that means that before formal discussions start or agendas circulate, each person present will speak, and all of us simply listen to where we each are at the moment. I saw how naturally the S.H.A.R.E.™ Tools fit with this idea, involving everyone, energizing each person as we listened, contributed, and created together.

I wish that Robert and I had had this set of intelligent yet simple conversation tools in our earlier international meetings. They clearly identify a missing link in communication that has the potential to solve today's most pressing global problems. As Albert Einstein said, "No problem can be solved with the same level of consciousness that created it." In the S.H.A.R.E.™ Tools, we have the new thinking that could revolutionize our interactions, elevating us to a place where everyone comes together as equals and creates the businesses and the world we all want, one conversation at a time.

INTRODUCTION

IF YOU ARE ANYTHING LIKE US, your life is filled with people, projects, goals, tasks, and dreams. And we're all trying to accomplish more in less time. We find ourselves seeking ways to create lives that work. It's a major challenge.

A big part of this challenge is trying to make our business lives more effective. Life in business can be dynamic and full of opportunity. But it can also be full of frustrating situations where momentum slows because of confusion about next steps, emotions heating up under stress, or well-meaning people working at cross-purposes.

None of us achieves our goals or dreams alone. We look to our coworkers, employees, employers, managers, leaders, clients, customers, family, and friends for assistance, ideas, encouragement, and advice. They look to us for the same. Everyone influences us and we influence them. The question is: how can we maximize our interactions and collaborations to meet and exceed our goals and theirs as well?

We do it by helping everyone get on the same page. And we do that by creating Revolutionary Conversations™ that empower us to embrace situations from more than just our perspective. The secret of these powerful conversations is the S.H.A.R.E.™ Tools you'll learn in this book. These five simple yet powerful interactive ingredients help us converse with others in a much more productive and successful way.

Not only do the S.H.A.R.E.™ Tools provide a conversational foundation that makes our own interactions more successful, but they also allow us to reach out to others and include them in the success and in the opportunity to make a difference in the world.

Originally developed for our UCLA Extension communication workshops and then used with enormous success in our business work, these Tools can help you navigate any conversation, whether you're in a packed boardroom or on a busy shop floor. By creating a distinctive connection between two or more people, they substantially increase communication's effectiveness. Here's a quick overview of how the S.H.A.R.E.™ Tools work:

1 STOP the conversation for clarity

2 HELP develop an environment for support and teamwork

3 ASK questions for better understanding

4 RISK presenting new ideas and options

5 EXPLORE ways to deliver collaborative results

We have experimented with, tested, and validated these Tools for more than twenty-five years and found that they really work. In fact, when we remember to use them, they seem to work every time.

We believe the S.H.A.R.E.™ Tools work for three reasons.

- **THEY'RE SIMPLE.** They make sense and they literally spell out the pure intent of communication: to SHARE and interact. Believe it or not, we didn't contrive to make the spelling turn out that way!

• THEY'RE FLEXIBLE. While one flows naturally into the other, you can also use them out of sequence and they still work. For instance, you can STOP and let people know you need to take a RISK—and they can embrace that and it can be quite successful. The Tools are also compatible with other communication and conversational approaches. They don't compete. If you're already a good listener, you'll become a better listener. If you're a good conversationalist, you'll add power and versatility to your existing skills.

• THEY OFFER A STRUCTURE FOR CONVERSATION. People can tell where they are and what to do to make the dialogue more effective for everyone. For instance, remembering STOP can help you stop yourself from talking too much, stop yourself from digressing, or stop someone else when you are uncertain. You always have a place to go—the Tools lead the way.

The Tools give you the power to create your conversational destiny. There's no more guessing—you have the Tools to make interaction more effective, alive, creative, productive, and successful. With that power comes more success for you and those around you.

Also, because you don't have to use the Tools perfectly, you can advance your goals and relationships at your own pace. Knowing you are moving forward, you can always circle back to issues and situations. As one of our S.H.A.R.E.® Workshop participants said: "Mark, you have a straightforward, profound way to break through conversation difficulties."

So far, we've stressed the benefits of these conversational dynamos from the individual's perspective. But there's a much more global application. We know firsthand that the Tools can have a major influence in helping businesses (in particular small- to medium-size businesses) be more successful, and there's a big reason why.

There's a "quiet crisis" in business today that's blocking opportunity and success and costing businesses billions.

According to the Gallup brochure *Employee Engagement,* "Actively disengaged employees erode an organization's bottom line, while breaking the spirits of colleagues in the process. Within the U.S. workforce, Gallup estimates this cost to be more than $300 billion in lost productivity alone." [http://www.slideshare.net/micje/employee-engagement-overview-brochure1]

What does this quiet crisis look like on a typical day? You see it in reduced productivity, increased customer complaints, decreased team cooperation, and frequent conflicts.

Whether you're a business owner or a team member trying to be successful, this environment of disengagement can take a tremendous toll. It can mean the difference between success and failure for individuals and businesses.

Revolutionary Conversations™ can combat this quiet crisis by *dramatically* changing a business's landscape, transforming a negative business culture and empowering individuals to work more effectively. Would you believe that you can do all of this simply by focusing on how people interact? We've seen it happen over and over in our consulting and teaching. Now we want to share it with you.

Mark's been consulting for more than thirty years. Most of that work has focused on helping companies navigate complicated business transitions—turnarounds, mergers, acquisitions—in order to grow and prosper. Much of the success stemmed from focusing on communications and on the quality of interactions between all of the business stakeholders. Getting everyone involved and invested in the process created better results, more satisfaction, and exceptional transformation by and for everyone.

While most of Mark's turnaround work is confidential, we can say that the Tools in this book were responsible, directly or indirectly, for these and other remarkable financial improvements:

- A distributor losing money, customers, and prestige goes from a $3 million loss to a $2 million profit, securing new customers and uniting the employees.

- A manufacturer doubles revenue from $3 million to $6 million as employees are engaged, trained, and empowered to do their jobs.

- A sales-order team, finally included, respected, and authorized to act, succeeds in helping retain almost 100% of the company's customers during an internal crisis.

- A struggling manufacturing firm doubles revenue and becomes highly profitable by partnering with customers to increase everyone's margins.

- A controller steps forward to help save the company by creating consensus, direction, and focus within the business.

- An accounts payable manager in a cash-challenged situation engages demanding vendors and radically shifts their perception of her company from "high risk" to "valued customer," a key factor in allowing the company to finally begin to resolve its cash-management problems.

The simple truth is that projects don't succeed unless conversations do. The transformation of our businesses and work life can begin with a single dialogue; an honest, collaborative interaction. These conversations can have big payoffs. A study from Towers Watson demonstrated that strong employee engagement levels can produce a 19% boost in productivity.

Revolutionary Conversations™ can supercharge a company's collective wisdom and assets. Whether initiated by a CEO, a manager, or a single employee, the S.H.A.R.E.™ Tools can help transform an organization of any size and expand opportunities for success—simply by having the right conversations, in the right way, at the right time.

We have always found that people achieve things as a group that they could never have achieved individually, if they can get on the same page and keep themselves there while going in the same direction. People on the line, those closest to the action, are repeatedly the most powerful users. They can often boost the organization and help create an environment where:

- loyalty goes both ways

- "actively attentive" team members replace the passive and zoned out

- creativity and enthusiasm checkmate fear and marginal thinking

- success is a reality for all: team members, owner/managers, customers, and all other stakeholders.

Are you ready for positive change and more powerful relationships? Try our Tools. We and many others have found that they produce the results we all seek. We've experienced how they create more meaning and more effectiveness, productivity, and success for all. We hope you find much value in our book.

REVOLUTIONARY CONVERSATIONS™

A S.H.A.R.E.™ BOOK

CHAPTER I

REVOLUTIONARY CONVERSATIONS™ WITH THE S.H.A.R.E.™ TOOLS

onversations aren't always easy. We've all experienced the difficulty of understanding and of being understood. We often find ourselves trying to understand others we've known for years!

Technology allows us to connect at lightning speed, but that doesn't necessarily mean that we understand each other better. In fact, the speed and volume of communication can put us on overload and introduce more confusion than clarity. We can be moving so quickly that we may gloss over meaning and understanding in favor of a quick sound bite. We need a more effective approach that provides fast, quantifiable results from authentic interactions.

A Revolutionary Conversation™ happens when we take the time—whether in a minute or an hour—to make sure we're all on the same page. When we do this, we create an environment of learning, not just knowing. In a learning environment, people can expand their understanding and also contribute more—often uncovering ideas, solutions, or opportunities that don't merely solve the problem, they maximize the result.

When we used the Tools in our consulting practices, we found they were adaptable to every sort of problem and pattern commonly found in business. There was enormous power in helping everyone stop what they were doing and truly engage each other—not make excuses, defend policies, protect alliances, posture, or hide behind the door, but truly interact—in a way that drove results.

Let's take a look at some of the results you can enjoy when you engage in Revolutionary Conversations™:

Higher Quality and Productivity

According to The Quality Portal http://thequalityportal.com/q_CoQ. htm, the "costs of poor quality can range from 15%–40% of business costs (e.g., rework, returns or complaints, reduced service levels, lost revenue)." So why don't we regularly stop for just a moment to make sure we're on the same page and going in the same direction? Because we're too busy getting things done—but are they really getting done?

One of the first things to do when helping a business handle a crisis situation is assess how individual departments share information within the department and with other departments. If, for instance, customer service and dispatch aren't using exactly the same information, how do the customers ever get what they need?

Here are some of the productivity challenges that have been addressed successfully on a regular basis using the S.H.A.R.E.™ Tools:

- **LOSE A DAY, LOSE A WEEK.** Projects of any kind always need to move forward. When we used the S.H.A.R.E.™ Tools, we could help move people off square one and out of stalemates.

- **OVERRELIANCE ON STREAMLINING.** Many businesses tend to think that organizational complexity can be solved by streamlining. That's sometimes part of the answer, but often it's a matter of getting the most from the people you have. The EXPLORE Tool engages everyone, accelerating productivity, efficiency, and creativity.

• LISTENING TO "YES" PEOPLE. In rough times, senior executives often find solace in the people who support their views, even if those views are unfounded. Leadership often expresses annoyance about the "complainers" on their staff. But we've found that workers who complain the most are sometimes the ones most engaged in the business, able to see what's really happening and disturbed by what they see. Taking time to seek HELP and to ASK what they observe, understand, and want to do can turn complaints into positive momentum.

• ANALYSIS PARALYSIS. Nothing will happen in business if people don't have a way to put tough issues on the table and resolve them. Over and over, we've found that profits come from profitable conversations: sharing information, directions, instructions, ideas, objections, concerns, confusions, and resolutions. And with the S.H.A.R.E.™ Tools, those conversations can happen not just in the boardroom, but also in offices, hallways, break rooms, washrooms, elevators, restaurants, cafeterias, convention rooms, on factory floors, showroom floors, airplanes, and every other place where people work together.

• "WHY DON'T THEY KEEP THEIR EYE ON THE BALL?" Our goal or agenda may be the most important thing on the planet, but if customer service staff hates their job and views the customer as the enemy, or if you haven't built support for a new system or policy implementation hasn't been established, good luck getting anything done. The Tools let you STOP and ask for HELP to make sure others are open to the priorities, understand them, and are all on the same page. You can also uncover what's holding things back, correct misperceptions, and advance the process.

• INNOVATION STAGNATION. A client once said he'd rather save a dollar than make three dollars. Many businesses in general shift to a focus on saving money, not making it. Cutting costs is useful, but gaining a competitive edge requires investing in the future. That means getting everyone engaged in innovation and implementing new ideas. The Tools let everyone RISK and EXPLORE new concepts.

• DISENGAGEMENT AND LOW MORALE. When we can't resolve issues, when mistakes and blame are common and relationships are built on internal political alignment, we disengage and perform at the "just getting by" level. This dissatisfaction with ourselves and our jobs feeds the quiet crisis we mentioned earlier that is undermining business success worldwide. The Tools can change this dynamic by building effective relationships among coworkers and helping them accomplish more each day. Connecting more fully to the organization helps break the downward spiral of disengagement and increases job and personal satisfaction.

Less Stress

Here's how a business owner who attended one of our S.H.A.R.E.® Workshops put it:

> *In the first week after attending your training, I used your method in mission-critical situations. It changed my world as I worked with my clients. Before the seminar, I would have stressed myself out trying to keep everybody happy, and that's no longer necessary. Amazing!*

At work we often feel we have to have all the answers—fast. It can be stressful and lead to unrealistic expectations, misinformation, and error. The Tools can help. Here's what one manager told us:

I just had a phone conversation with a client who always wants to ask me "just one quick question." He talks very fast and wants a black-or-white answer. He wasn't giving me enough information for me to be sure about the facts. I did a STOP and asked if he could HELP me out and clarify something he was telling me. It worked GREAT! The best part is that I remembered to STOP and ASK for HELP. Hurray!

This kind of dynamic goes on everywhere in business. We get into less-than-good patterns with people and make do. It could be with a customer, an employee, fellow team members, or the boss. But see how quickly this manager could start the shift to a whole new way to work together! It sure beats getting stressed-out or angry and maybe saying: "I can't answer rapid-fire questions. Maybe this isn't working." This manager had a Revolutionary Conversation™ by using the Tools to be open to her client's needs and respectful of her own knowledge and skill, so that an appropriate solution could emerge.

More Collaboration, Less Competition

The Tools can help us avoid the "my idea/your idea" trap. Instead, we can achieve new levels of interaction, capturing more opportunities and more success. The Tools create a framework for considering everyone's contributions and helping us all to contribute honestly.

The Tools also tap into what pioneering management consultant Mary Parker Follett called "The Law of the Situation." Follett was a leader in the development of the concept of management in the 1920s. Often called the "Prophet of Management" (also the title of her biography), she was a major influence on renowned management thought leader Peter Drucker, who wrote the introduction to her biography. Here's a summary of her landmark definition:

THE LAW OF THE SITUATION: A DEFINITION

> *Human relations school of management concept that conflicts should be resolved according to the facts of the situation and not by reference to the relative superiority of any party over the other. In other words, the search for solutions to management problems should be governed by the demands of the situation and not by reference to any authority or principle.*
>
> –Proposed by the U.S. management philosopher Mary Parker Follett (1868–1933). [http://www.businessdictionary.com/definition/law-of-the-situation.html].

The key here is that Follett's ideas and in particular the Law of the Situation and another concept called Power With versus Power Over are the baseline for most of the insightful and major changes in business today. The S.H.A.R.E.™ Tools give us the "how" for manifesting these core ideas in everyday life on the job, helping us tap into the wealth of information and knowledge that exists within all situations and releasing the capability of a situation to solve itself.

The Tools have helped coauthor Barbara release the power of the Law of the Situation in her public relations business:

> *In the past when I would give potential clients my "instant ideas," the energy in the room immediately changed. They'd stop talking about what they needed and start tell-*

ing me why my ideas wouldn't work! I discovered that nodding my head worked better than words—it told them I was listening! I always got new clients when I would ASK for clarity and HELP in understanding their needs and objectives. They signed up because they knew I had really heard them.

The S.H.A.R.E.™ Tools have revolutionized the outcomes of all sorts of common business challenges. Our S.H.A.R.E.® Workshops have shown that participants are so eager and confident that they immediately use them to address their difficult situations:

- **disgruntled customers/clients**
- **thorny negotiation**
- **angry associates**
- **demanding individuals**
- **nonstop talkers**

The S.H.A.R.E.™ Tools can work at home, too. One of our seminar students announced, "The Tools worked so well at work that I tried it with my wife. We were able to talk about subjects we had never been able to bring up before. This allowed us to create a new life for ourselves."

Starting Your Own Revolutionary Conversations™

What if you could embrace two Revolutionary Conversations™ a day? What could happen if you could STOP a client from steamrolling over you, ASK an employee to HELP you understand how you could work better with each other, ASK your supervisor more questions about your new job duties, RISK bringing the real story to the board so that meaningful changes could be made, and EXPLORE how your ideas for a new product could have substantial impact on the company? Wouldn't that be exceptional?

Revolutionary Conversations™ need not be spectacular to be productive. They do, however, need to be genuine—not just forums for steering others in our direction or way of thinking—and they need to help everyone shift their patterns a bit so that new, more productive ways and ideas can surface.

We love how Mark Twain put it: "Let us make a special effort to stop communicating with each other, so we can have some conversation."

The foundations that make Revolutionary Conversations™ possible include:

- **Coming alongside others to avoid "my idea/your idea."**

- **Seeking to find out "what happened?" not "who's to blame?"**

- **Understanding that what makes us successful is not what we know, but what we need to know.**

- **Avoiding "telling" and focusing on a collaborative/ contributory approach with others.**

- **Acknowledging your own and others' contributions along the way.**

- **Letting others clearly understand and appreciate that you want to collaborate and engage.**

Whether it's two minutes at the water cooler or two hours in a make-or-break crisis meeting, using the S.H.A.R.E.™ Tools in conversations can bring surprising results at times when you really need them—and at times when you least expect them, they can help establish a foundation to create a whole new way of doing things. Let's take a look at them in more detail.

THE S.H.A.R.E.™ Tools: An Overview

STOP

We can use STOP to get a good start in a conversation by ensuring that we have the correct information. STOP can be beneficial when conversation conditions change and you need to get clarification, catch your breath, or change the direction from monologue to dialogue. STOP can slow down a conversation if we're getting lost or politely put the brakes on a runaway speaker.

You can use STOP externally when you need clarification. You can use STOP internally when you see the possibility of trouble if you keep going down the same conversational path. STOP is not used to grab the conversation by cutting off someone else, but it can be a critical part of advancing any conversation in a productive way. STOP is a beginning, and it works even better with its counterpart HELP.

HELP

STOP and HELP go together. You almost can't have one without the other. We use them when we want to be sure we're on track: we STOP someone to get HELP in understanding the information, the situation, or the meaning of what is being said.

STOP without a request for HELP could be considered rude, but using STOP and HELP together begins to build an atmosphere of cooperation. They change the conversation dynamic by encouraging people to engage in the process.

HELP expands and deepens the avenues to new information—and remember, success isn't what you know, but what you need to know. It shifts us from inquisitor to collaborator. Once you STOP the conversation and create a HELP environment, you and your conversational partners can ASK questions from a comfort zone: you are in this together.

ASK

Once you STOP someone and acknowledge that you need HELP, you can use ASK to clarify and expand the facts and ideas in the situation. You can use STOP–HELP–ASK until you know that you are on the same page and you feel that everyone (including you!) has a clear understanding and some communication momentum.

ASK is not an interrogative exercise of "you ask and I answer." It's an expansive, fluid process to uncover more potential in a conversation, making it more robust and productive. Then when you're ready to introduce a new idea, you move to RISK.

RISK

RISK allows you to introduce new ideas. Like the other steps, RISK is a two-way bridge: it carries us into EXPLORE, but we can move back into STOP, HELP, and ASK if the going gets rough or whenever clarification is needed.

RISK is also an action point. When you RISK bringing up a new idea, a different point of view, or a difficult topic, there is the possibility for the conversation to move to a higher level, to advance the process and to get things done: "Bob, your questions have stimulated a new idea. Do you think we can talk about it?" If the group or your conversation partner is open to something new, you're ready to advance to EXPLORE. But always remember that you can go back to STOP–HELP–ASK if others aren't ready to go with you down a new path.

The groundwork you've laid through STOP–HELP–ASK can mitigate challenges in RISK and help prevent others being caught off guard by an idea or subject out of left field. By the time you reach RISK, everyone will have a better understanding of the situation and enough information to make intelligent suggestions. You can use

STOP–HELP–ASK to get more details about any challenges or misunderstandings. Move to EXPLORE when you hear, "Hey, good idea! Let's see how we can make it work."

EXPLORE

With EXPLORE, you are able to create new ideas, solve problems, and look at things from new perspectives. When you interact in EXPLORE, you'll be able to leverage the knowledge and experience that everyone can offer. This is a powerful place to be. It can be highly energizing. As always, you can return to STOP–HELP–ASK to keep the conversation on track and everyone on the same page.

Many participants have jumped right in to use the Tools, and others have taken their time. One student said, "Finally, I used STOP, and it changed the whole meeting! I can't wait to try the other Tools." We find that as people become more comfortable using the Tools for daily challenges, they begin to expand their horizons to more creative possibilities:

- seeking new ideas to increase effectiveness and success

- initiating creative conversations to resolve impasses

- agreeing on important financial considerations, such as collection of overdue debts

- advancing major concepts, such as introducing the board to the idea of merging with or acquiring another business

- constructively confronting troubling situations such as challenges in team meetings

- resolving mistakes

- giving/receiving bad news

- discussing a raise

- closing a sale

- . . . and more!

We are constantly amazed at how effective these Tools can be in the most difficult of situations. Even when a small number of people are trained in the S.H.A.R.E.™ Tools, the rate of project success increases substantially. Better yet, their colleagues learn the Tools through association. This creates a Language for Success™—a way of conversing—that minimizes distractions and misunderstandings. End result: better ideas, more collaboration, and the power and ability to get things done.

As business focuses globally, we need to confront what we know about everything. That means being involved, asking questions, seeking help, knowing when we don't know, and collaborating so everyone can help. No more heroes who think they know all the answers!

We need people working together, engaged and succeeding as they are appreciated. The S.H.A.R.E.™ Tools can lead the way. We believe that *Revolutionary Conversations*™ can make a substantial contribution to the world of business and the individuals in it.

How to Use This Book

In the chapters that follow, we provide the S.H.A.R.E.™ Tools with observations and examples from our business and personal experiences, plus practical scenarios showing how these Tools might be used in your conversations. We use simple examples of common workplace experiences to make the Tools easier to learn and remember when you need them most. Every day we are all confronted with situations that are surprises, immediate in nature and critical to relationships and productivity for today and tomorrow. It's the chance conversation at the water cooler, the new customer or client with unexpected demands, the employee who breaks down, the emergency on the shop floor, the manager who quits out of nowhere— these spontaneous events can catch us off guard. In these kinds of situations, we need to quickly access the S.H.A.R.E.™ Tools. Accordingly, many of the examples in this book are easy to remember and put into practice.

We've also included more sophisticated situations and actual case studies to let you see the full range of the Tools in sections called S.H.A.R.E.™ Tools in Action. Of course, multiple management, corporate finance, and reengineering strategies and other problem-solving soft technologies were at work to successfully resolve these situations. The Tools fit smoothly into all kinds of business challenges to enhance their success.

As you practice the Tools and they become a natural part of your conversation, you'll be able to draw on them in more demanding situations. You'll find that Revolutionary Conversations™ can happen anytime, anywhere.

So, please read and learn about the Tools. Then start practicing! STOP even if you leave skid marks on the boss's hardwood floors, seek HELP in the easiest and most honest way, ASK questions with an open mind and heart, RISK when you see that a reward for all may be around the corner, and EXPLORE as others begin to come alongside.

We're confident that you will soon have your own Revolutionary Conversations™ to share with your colleagues and friends.

All the best and enjoy.

CHAPTER 2

STOP—THE ART OF STOPPING TO GO FORWARD

A stop sign is intended to keep traffic moving safely. It works because it's based on a mutual understanding of the protocols of stop signs and traffic laws. STOP within the S.H.A.R.E.™ Tools is a potent word that positions us for success because it is a constructive interruption that creates an opportunity for understanding.

The purpose of STOP is to be sure the conversation is on track and advancing the process. This is not, "Stop, I want to talk!" The S.H.A.R.E.™ STOP is intended to help you or others catch a breath, clear up confusion, gather thoughts, and move the conversation forward. It's a signal to all that we might need to get more on the same page and begin to come alongside each other.

A managing partner of a professional services firm observed that STOP shows respect for others and honors their power in conversations. She uses STOP often to make sure clients understand the technical aspects of their discussions. She STOPs herself and then the discussion as she feels the technical information getting a bit overwhelming. She knows it is important for everyone to be clear.

Let's look at some situations where a constructive pause can make a difference.

A Little HELP Here, Please! Let's STOP to Understand

Life in the workplace is busy. We interact with many different people in myriad situations. The pace of work is accelerating, directions change constantly without warning, and developing situations require new instructions. To survive and succeed, we must course correct for rapidly changing conditions. Knowing how to communicate and receive new information quickly and accurately is essential. Most of us, to save face or to save time, have said "I understand" when, in fact, we may have no idea of what is happening. Sometimes, we get lucky and figure things out, but at other times we can end up making costly or time-consuming mistakes.

As previously noted the cost of inferior work can span 15% to 40% of business costs. Most businesses don't know what their quality costs are because they don't keep reliable statistics. But finding and correcting mistakes consumes an inordinately large portion of resources. Typically, the cost to eliminate a failure in the customer phase is five times greater than it is at the development or manufacturing phase.

See if this scenario sounds familiar. Senior manager Andrew is giving instructions about a complicated project to his department, now seated around the conference table. Everyone is taking notes furiously because Andrew is hard on those who can't keep up with his fast-paced style. In general, people don't bother him with questions; many times, they've huddled after meetings to figure things out. After the meeting ends, everyone heads for the door—except for Eric, a new team member who recently joined the company. Eric has decided to STOP and ASK, "Andrew, do you have a moment? I'm not sure I understand precisely how. . . ." Eric then goes through his checklist of pertinent questions and asks for clarification on details for handling the project.

While the rest of the team tries to figure things out, Eric has taken the opportunity to talk with Andrew to be sure he doesn't waste time by guessing what needs to happen. It's important to note that Eric's STOP for clarification isn't a substitute for paying attention. He paid close attention during the meeting and identified key areas where he needed more detail. Through his well-thought-out questions, Eric demonstrates that he's focused on getting the job done in the most effective way possible. When Eric starts his part of the project, he knows what's expected.

This type of situation happens every day in business and in our personal lives. Eric's STOP was simple, but it brings value to both Eric and the business. Getting the project done quickly and well can save time and money. It will save Eric (and Andrew) frustration. It will demonstrate Eric's value to the business. And, as an extra bonus for the business, Eric sets an example for others. Eric also benefits personally by being better at his job and taking more satisfaction in his work, which can boost his career and compensation. Such a small action, with such big results!

Andrew has an opportunity to use STOP, too, instead of quickly giving instructions and rushing people out the door. The purpose of giving instructions is to get things done. Giving and receiving instructions is actually a collaborative endeavor, and to be most successful it needs to be interactive and focused on what needs to happen. Spending a few extra minutes to make sure everyone's on the same page results in increased efficiency over the course of the project. So, let's do an instant replay.

Andrew could STOP himself to check with the group to be sure they understand his instructions and to find out if they have questions. He would not say, "Do you understand?" because most employees (wanting to impress him) would say yes, whether they did or not. What he might say is:

- "Let me STOP here to be sure we're all tracking."

- "I've been talking a lot and I want to STOP to be sure this is making sense."

By taking responsibility for his communication with this approach, Andrew can protect the business from mistakes, wasted time, and overruns. The upfront investment of time quickly translates directly to the bottom line. With a clear understanding of the project, employees can work more effectively as a team. Strong team structures support employee retention. All of that equates to greater profitability.

STOP to Stay Focused

STOP can help keep everyone focused and on task by pulling all back to where everybody is at their best: in the present, here and now. There are several easy ways to do this:

- Listen to what others are saying by internally repeating their words. This is beneficial when you've had a busy day and think you can't listen to another person wanting or needing anything from you. Repeating their words internally can help you slow down and focus. Another technique is to watch the person's lips while they're speaking.

• Take notes to focus on capturing key elements of what the speaker has to say. That way, you have an easy reminder of key points.

• Make mental notes of key words, phrases, or concepts by "parking" them internally. This approach keeps you attentive and ready to engage as appropriate. This is about finding out what is going on, not about formulating rebuttals.

• Observe and internally acknowledge body language, facial expression, and other nuances without judgment. Pay attention to find out more about what is happening without engaging or making comments or drawing conclusions. To stay present, avoid judgment and criticism. When you begin to make internal judgments, it is a signal to STOP and get back to the present. If you start to analyze, you will go down another path and lose focus, and you will no longer be attentive to the conversation.

• STOP and let others know if/when the gist of the dialogue has been lost. At those times, your partners in conversation can help get you back on board.

• STOP yourself to stay in the present. Be conscious that using STOP to stay in the game is essential to greater success in all forms of conversation and communication.

STOP to Discover Opportunities

Years ago, Mark was working with a client to collect a substantial sum of money from one of her customers. After months of posturing, they met in her attorney's office to discuss resolving this equitably. Present at the meeting with Mark were his client and her attorney, her customer and his attorney, and a third-party attorney with interest in the collection of this receivable.

Mark's attention was focused on where he could add value without getting in the way of others. There were several deeply conflicting agendas in that meeting—not unusual in many interpersonal situations, especially legal negotiations. This conversation was about collecting as much as possible versus paying nowhere near what was owed.

The customer had a story to tell, and he wanted his questions answered before any discussion of paying bills. As Mark watched and listened, he focused on understanding what each person said, trying to see if a bridge could be built between the parties.

As Mark listened to the customer, it was clear that he was honest, thoughtful, and committed to doing the right thing. Mark also noticed that the customer kept referring to a list he had of invoices previously received. The customer could not understand why and how additional bills were being presented.

With an opening to STOP the conversation, Mark interrupted, "Jim, can we STOP a minute? Could you HELP? If I could ASK you a few questions, I would appreciate it." As Mark said this, he leaned forward and reached his hands to the middle of the conference table to get the customer's attention. With his agreement, Mark asked, "Could I look at the list you just mentioned?"

As Mark looked at the list, he commented, "This is only about twenty-five percent of the total that is unpaid and owed to my client. I'm confused." Jim replied, "That's what I don't understand. I have a conflict with some of the bills she's presenting." Mark offered, "Would it be too forward of me to assume that you agree that the bills on your list are unpaid, and those are ready for your payment?" "You're correct," Jim agreed, "but I still haven't gotten answers to my questions." Mark's next question was: "If we were to prioritize the other bills and come to a number that you could accept, would that move this process forward?" "Yes," Jim said, "Could you do that for me?" Mark's client gladly agreed and committed to get Jim's questions answered.

When they walked out of that meeting, they were unanimously on track to get their problems resolved in the near future. By staying in the present, focusing on what was going on, and using several STOP techniques to keep on task, they were able to begin to resolve this stalemate. STOP was there for Mark again and again as everyone worked together to accomplish what Mark had come there to do: to get his client paid and not create a distraction or go down another unproductive path. Again, STOP saves the day!

STOP to Deal with Emotions

Our emotions can take over a conversation without our uttering a word. As a conversation unfolds, we experience a constant stream of emotions in response to what's being said. Of course, so does the other person! Sometimes, our emotions stem from what the other person is saying or doing. At other times, our own thoughts take us down a distracting path. Here are some examples of thoughts that trigger emotions during conversations:

- **"What did I do? Am I getting fired?"**

- **"If he does that again, I'm going to . . . "**

- **"I don't like where this conversation is headed."**

Emotions can interrupt our ability to listen and participate in the conversation. We start listening to our emotions and are no longer engaged in the conversation. And this can happen to the other person as well!

STOP gives us a way to stay with the words, not get caught up in

the emotions. We can use STOP to protect ourselves from someone who is confronting us. We can use STOP for ourselves before
we say or do something that we can't take back or fix. We can use
STOP to save someone else from letting his or her emotions take
over.

In emotional situations, some of us get mad and say so; others of
us draw the Teflon cape around ourselves and say "whatever" and
hope the storm passes; still others are like terrified deer in the head-
lights. Regardless of how well planned your strategy is, when emotions run high, those plans may not stand a chance. Don't let fear or
anger prevent you from participating productively in conversations.
Here are some examples of how STOP can create opportunities for
change in emotional situations.

The Confrontational Boss (or Employee!)

Tom was a boss with a fiery temper that he didn't control. Mary
reported directly to him. She was a bright, intelligent, experienced
manager, but she was terrified of Tom when he was angry, which was
much too often. Contributions she might have made were not offered
because her fears overwhelmed her.

Tom had a habit of storming into her office, yelling about client
problems. She would stammer and withdraw; then try to fix everything. The toll on her was so significant that she was beginning to feel
the impact on her health. Mary needed some way to protect herself
from these verbal onslaughts, so we started working with her one-
on-one on using the S.H.A.R.E.™ Tools. First, she needed a way to
respond when Tom came storming in. For that, Mary needed STOP
twice. The first STOP was for herself—to catch her breath, master her
own fear, and find her voice. Once she had managed her emotional
response to the situation, she could find a way to STOP Tom mid-

yell. Doing this wasn't easy. When an emotional response is so powerful, it can take courage to try something new. But Mary decided she had nothing to lose. If her boss was already yelling, she figured things couldn't get any worse!

The good news is that, by combining STOP with a request for HELP, Mary was able to interrupt her boss's tirade. When she found her voice after a STOP, she could ask:

"Wait a minute. Can we look at what the client said so I can understand?"

The interaction between Tom and Mary began to change. Once she was able to break through her fear of his yelling, Mary found herself to be much more confident and able to articulate her thoughts more clearly. Her knowledge and talents weren't lost because of her reaction to Tom.

As Mary began to contribute more, Tom and others in the business realized what an asset she was. Several months after she started practicing her new skills, Mary was promoted several levels. Since then, she has expanded her career into a whole new area of the business. It's a wonderful success story that can happen to any of us if we're willing to try the Tools.

Mary also contributed to Tom's success. Thanks to her use of STOP to prevent him from going overboard in his anger, he began to be aware of his power to STOP himself. Whether he was conscious of it or not, his anger had stood in the way of his success. As Tom learned ways to work with people without losing his temper, he became a more effective manager.

For both Mary and Tom, STOP brought value. The evolving dynamic between them began to change the culture of the business. In the end, Mary's STOP contributed to making the company a better place to work and added value for every person there.

I'm So Angry, I Could . . .

Imagine you've come from a lovely lunch with someone you enjoy. You hand the valet your parking ticket. The valet cannot find your keys . . . slight uptick to irritation. Eventually, he finds your keys, but the car still hasn't been brought around after ten minutes . . . increasing emotional uptick to aggravation. Finally, he pulls up in your car, and you see a scratch down the length of the passenger side . . . aggravation skyrockets to full-blown anger.

As difficult as it may be, you need an internal STOP to get in control of your anger. Your emotions are real, but acting on them won't fix the car, improve your day, or make a positive difference with the valet. So STOP—get control of the emotions before you do anything. Rather than an angry tirade, you might say:

"Whoa! I see a big scratch on my car. I don't want to get angry, but I need to find out what happened and what we can do."

We've all experienced situations or relationships at work or in life that have made us angry. It's not easy to manage circumstances if emotions get in the way. Before you consider giving up on these situations or relationships, take a look at what happened with a colleague of ours.

Jay, a consultant who has worked with the S.H.A.R.E.™ Tools over the years, has always been especially attentive to the quality of his client service, going above and beyond to support his clients' success. But in this instance, he found himself in a difficult spot. He had started working with a new client on a complicated project. In the beginning, it sounded profitable and exciting for everyone.

Then, something changed. The project started to slide downhill. Next, there were questions about Jay's experience. Then a list of complaints was documented by e-mail, and he started getting defensive. Jay joined with another manager at the firm to offer a detailed rebuttal in defense of his own actions and the firm's position. This was not received well by the client.

On a Friday afternoon, Jay received a termination notice from the client. At this point, STOP kicked in for him. He realized that he had been reacting and fighting, not thinking and learning.

First, Jay engaged the S.H.A.R.E.™ Tools internally.

- **STOP: "I need to slow down."**

- **HELP: "I need some HELP here."**

- **ASK: "What can I do in this situation?"**

Then, he created a checklist of what he knew and didn't know about this situation. By doing this, he calmed down and realized that he must call his now-former client and discuss his termination.

During the call, Jay let the client know he was concerned and would appreciate an opportunity to talk. The client agreed, and they set an appointment for Monday.

That's great, you may be thinking. But what if the client had responded to Jay's STOP this way: "I don't see the point of talking. I don't have anything more to say about this. I'm very clear about my perspective. We terminated the relationship because we weren't happy with your performance and we don't think you're up for the job. I think we both should move on."

If that had happened, Jay would have needed to keep his anger from resurfacing with an internal STOP first. Then he could have used another STOP with the client: "I'm shocked and confused. Could we talk about this? Your HELP would be appreciated." Jay's intent would have been to use HELP to understand and clarify the situation, and then bridge to the possibility of working with the client to discuss miscommunication during the project that might have pushed things off track.

As Jay prepared for the Monday teleconference, he reviewed what had transpired with this client and the project. Then he set everything aside and went camping for the weekend. This was another important STOP for him. By getting completely away from the situation, he prevented himself from dwelling on Monday's conference and letting anger reignite and get the better of him.

We don't always have opportunities to take a break in situations like this, but when your emotions flare, try to get time and distance from the situation if you can. Consider even taking a few minutes for a walk around the block. This physical and emotional STOP can assist you in managing the next conversation more effectively.

Jay arrived on Monday with a positive attitude and a goal to have a meaningful, productive dialogue with his client. He reviewed his notes and made a list of questions and some ideas about what had happened. He prepared himself to be open and listen to whatever he would hear from the client.

In their call, he told the client that he wanted to talk so that both of them could understand and have clarity. He added that as part of this conversation, they might discover what could have been done to prevent the present situation. He did STOP himself from defending. He secured the client's HELP and permission to ASK questions. With his open-ended questions (more about these in the ASK chapter), he saw how he had gone down the wrong path.

Realizing that he and the client were really beginning to communicate, Jay chose to take a RISK. He asked if he could share how he had envisioned the project and how he felt communications between them could have transpired. Because he had set the stage for cooperation with STOP–HELP–ASK, the client was open to the information he wanted to present.

As the conversation continued, they realized that both had misunderstandings. The client said, "I need to think about all this. Can we talk in a week? We might be able to rebuild our relationship." This was an appropriate STOP for the client. "Absolutely," Jay replied, "Should I wait for your call?" The client said, "No, please call me next Wednesday morning."

Jay got off the phone with a clear realization of what a difference STOP could make in a client relationship. He'd used the S.H.A.R.E.™ Tools to gain the opportunity to win back the client and begin rebuilding that relationship. Even if he hadn't been able to win back the client (which he did) and they had parted ways, things would have ended on a positive note with everyone learning and growing.

There was more. Jay felt great after having turned around the situation. That positive energy was a factor in his securing a new client later in the day! And it all started with STOP.

Jay's experience shows that it's never too late to improve a challenging situation, and that when we succeed, there's no knowing where the good results will lead. The S.H.A.R.E.™ Tools can give us the road map to get there.

I Feel Like . . .

When we hear hurtful words or someone behaves in a way that causes us pain, we can use STOP to connect to the situation in a way that gives us a buffer. As Mary did with her confrontational boss, first, STOP yourself. You may need to STOP yourself from lashing out or from pretending it doesn't matter. Either way, a STOP is in order. First, STOP to control your response; then find a way to STOP the other person. Once you STOP what's happening in the moment, you can change the pattern of the conversation and have a chance to change things going forward. You might say:

"Please STOP. I need to understand this. Can you HELP me understand why you feel that way?"

Emotional situations and strong feelings happen. It's amazing what using STOP can do to keep reactions from escalating. Like a stop sign that makes drivers stop accelerating and look both ways to see where everyone else is before moving, STOP in conversations allows us to regroup, see where everyone is, and find a way to help the conversation stay in a positive direction.

We were working with a business that was experiencing significant change. The management team wasn't working well together and tempers were running hot. We had been integrating the S.H.A.R.E.™ Tools into the change process, and some team members were practicing them. When we came back for a follow-up meeting, the controller told us this story.

"I was working on a tight deadline preparing a detailed financial report when Harold, my accounting manager, came into my office unannounced, upset about some financial data and demanding my immediate attention. My mind went blank for a moment. Then, the Tools kicked in and I knew that if I could STOP myself from reacting, I could find out what was happening. I did STOP myself so quickly that there were practically skid marks on the desk! Then I said, 'Harold, can we STOP a minute? Please sit down. Can you HELP me understand what's going on?' Later, I realized how powerful it is to STOP myself. In a situation that could get out of control, the one person I know I can control is me. Once I get my wits together, I can approach the situation from a different perspective."

Since then, this controller has taken on more responsibility inside the organization because of his ability to handle difficult situations. Part of his strength comes from his ability to first apply the internal STOP; then, to take action. His presence of mind enhances his career opportunities and also serves as a powerful role model, demonstrating a different way to manage emotional situations. Now, instead of tempers being hot, collaborative problem resolution is hot!

The Complete STOP—Exit Stage Left

Sometimes, despite our best efforts, we find that it's impossible to make a connection with someone. One or both people may have such intense emotions about an issue or situation that no common ground can be reached. It's OK to end the conversation completely. STOP allows us to postpone a conversation that's not going anywhere or if it's inappropriate at the moment.

Suppose you have an unhappy customer on the phone. You've used STOP to help redirect the situation toward a more cooperative interaction. Still, things have escalated. Now you've used STOP on yourself so that you don't yell back. At this point, you may decide it's best to end the conversation and schedule a time to come back to it later. You might say:

"Mr. Peterson, I need to slow down [STOP]. I need to get more information so I can resolve this issue with you. Can we talk later today? May I call you at three p.m.?"

If Mr. Peterson is still upset and perhaps using language he learned sailing around the world, then you can assert your rights appropriately and disconnect with a Complete STOP:

"Mr. Peterson, I need to STOP this conversation now. I'm hanging up and will call you later in the day to discuss this issue."

The Complete STOP protects you and Mr. Peterson from further damage. Both of you need time to gather your composure. You add value by taking responsibility for the situation, creating the possibility of getting back on track at a later time.

A Complete STOP may be in order if you realize that your own emotions are running high during a conversation. STOP yourself and ask whether you and the other person should talk later. Take the time you need so that you can come back to the conversation with the S.H.A.R.E.™ Tools ready to go.

STOP Tips

STOP is more an art than a science. We like to think of it as the art of constructive interruption. We often mention the act of coming alongside others as an important aspect of helping the S.H.A.R.E.™ Tools work. Well, STOP is a way you can really come alongside yourself and make the most of your conversational skills, your professional abilities, and what others can contribute as well. STOP helps protect and advance the process for everyone.

Below are some STOP Tips to get you started. As you practice the art of constructive interruption, it will become easier and you'll find your own creative ways to STOP.

Spotting the Signals

One of the best ways to STOP is to recognize the signals that STOP should be in your future. Maybe you're losing focus, getting tired, feeling distracted, becoming angry, getting too animated, talking too much, worrying about an issue, feeling confused, and on and on. These and many other signals are great STOP cues. You can make a short list of your own personal triggers that remind you to STOP. Here are some internal signals that we may be rambling too long:

- **FEELING SHORT OF BREATH.** When we're talking as fast as possible, we tend to run out of breath. If you feel breathless, it's probably time to do an internal STOP.

- **LOSING OUR TRAIN OF THOUGHT.** Our ideas may not be well connected. We may not remember where we started. If you're wondering how you got to a statement you made, STOP yourself to reflect, then move forward to get HELP, perhaps by requesting that others summarize.

- **BEING SO EXCITED OR EMOTIONAL THAT WE TALK TOO FAST.** If you find yourself stumbling over words or talking over others, it's time to take a break and get someone else into the conversation. You may not have to do a Complete STOP. Simply slowing down the pace of your delivery can make the difference in whether your audience can follow you or not.

It's also important that we take responsibility to STOP ourselves to be sure that our conversation partner is tracking with us. Look for signals: people's reactions to what's going on, the comments and the body language of those around you, the level of stress in a situation, the amount of time that something is taking, to name some. Stopping yourself and others is so valuable that it's well worth the effort to pay attention to your own and others' signals and let them guide you to a better and more productive conversation. If internal bells don't go off, you can be sure that your audience, be it 1 or 1,000, will definitely give you the signal that it's time to STOP. Watch or listen for the following signs:

- Your listener hasn't said much for a while.

- Your audience's eyes have that distant or "glazed over" look.

- Your audience is staring at you, but you can't tell if it's out of interest or frustration.

- Your listener is toying with a pencil, pocket change, or some other object.

- Your listener is staring at the cell phone, willing it to ring, or busily texting someone to call as soon as possible.

Challenges to Putting the Brakes on Yourself

Sometimes we can be incredibly clueless when it comes to putting the brakes on ourselves. Here are some ways we trip ourselves up:

- We want to give as much information as possible in a small amount of time, and we forget that the listener may not have time to understand it or make significant connections. We think that, if we just keep talking, others will catch up and start following us. Don't count on it. People who are lost often put their energy into pretending to understand, rather than concentrating on what others are saying. Or they may be working on a challenging rebuttal of what they think is being said. Better to STOP and find out if everyone understands each other.

• We don't want to lose our train of thought, so we keep talking. We can STOP briefly to acknowledge that someone has a question and request permission to finish our thought. With permission given, we can wrap up the thought and then STOP for the question.

• We want to get something on the table. Sometimes, we dump our concerns with a thud on our listener's shoulders. Take this sense of urgency to sound off as a signal to STOP yourself to be sure your listener is ready to receive what you have to say.

• We're under the delusion that everyone is fascinated because they're staring at us. We need to STOP ourselves and turn to the audience for HELP. "I'm wondering if there are any questions I need to address?" It's important that if you notice something isn't working, you need to STOP yourself and turn to the audience for HELP.

• We're afraid to lose the floor to another speaker. By graciously yielding the floor, we gain a conversation partner who may do the same for us, since people tend to model the behavior of others during conversations. And if you do lose the flow, you can go back to STOP again and regroup.

• We doubt that others could have anything interesting to add. You'll never know if you don't find out!

• We want to keep control of the conversation. A conversation controlled by one person is usually short and may not result in consensus or in anything new.

The Graceful STOP for Yourself

When you get a signal from your listener (or from yourself) that you need a STOP, avoid saying something like, "You're not getting this, are you?" To sensitive ears, this can sound like, "How could a nitwit like you understand a genius like me?" Consider a more gracious STOP:

• "I need to slow down."

• "I've been talking a while."

• "Oops, can we STOP for a second?"

• "I sense I am being confusing. I want to STOP to find out if that's true."

• "Let's STOP a moment to discuss any problems or concerns that are coming to mind."

• "Does this make sense to you? I feel I need to STOP to check in."

• "I am going to STOP. I need your HELP to get your feedback and/or questions."

• "I'm not sure I have all the information. Can we STOP and clarify what's been said?"

A gracious STOP genuinely seeks HELP, inviting others to join the conversation for collaboration and understanding. With everyone in the conversation, the team grows stronger and the solutions more effective.

Gracefully Helping Others STOP

The opening line of a graceful STOP is important because it assures others that you're not trying to take the conversation ball away; you simply want more information to better understand their point. Try some of these ideas:

- "Excuse me. May I STOP you for a moment?"

- "I'm sorry to interrupt, but I'm not sure I understand. Are you saying . . . ?"

- "I'm interested, but I'm not sure I've got it . . . "

- "Oops, wait a minute. I'm lost here . . . "

- "Hold that thought, please. I want to understand what you mean by . . . "

- "Just a moment. Could we talk about this?"

- "Could we slow the pace? I'm losing the thread of the conversation."

How would you respond to these if you were the speaker? It's the graciousness of the STOP that makes the difference: it makes a speaker receptive to pausing so you can understand and verify his or her meaning.

The Group STOP for Everyone

We have a client who, as her company's chief operating officer and a faithful S.H.A.R.E.™ Tools user, has taken the STOP to a group level. Her business has many high-stress deadlines. Sometimes emotions run high and accusations can fly. She knows that this is counter-productive for everyone. Often when she uses the Group STOP, she announces that they will take a walk around the building, and she leads the way. Fortunately, they're located in a climate where that can happen year-round. This Complete STOP for the group breaks the tension by removing people from the situation for a few minutes. Everyone has a moment to take a breath, gather thoughts, and release tensions that can build under demanding deadlines. Following their walk, they regroup, address issues, create a solution, and move on.

Conversations are full of curves, surprises, slippery slopes, and uphill battles. STOP is the first Tool in getting everyone on solid footing. You can use it anytime—for yourself or for others. It can be gracious and effective. It can save you and others from accelerating into situations that are difficult to handle. If STOP is the only S.H.A.R.E.™ Tool you use, you'll still be well on your way to improving every conversation.

S.H.A.R.E.™ Tools in Action

How STOP Delivered the Message

Our client was a family-owned specialty manufacturing company. The business had done well, but for reasons the owners hadn't been able to figure out, it was beginning to lose money. They feared that if this trend continued, they would soon be in real trouble.

We requested that a core group of managers and owners complete a confidential written survey. The survey responses were stunning and filled with negativity.

In these kinds of projects, it's important to share information in such a way that no one can spot who said what. What a job that was in this case! This information was highly inflammatory and accusatory. It would be challenging to present this information so it could be used constructively. There was also the RISK that the client might dismiss us for being the messenger, even though they needed to hear the reality of things.

When the day of our presentation arrived, we still hadn't come up with a comfortable approach. But as we walked into the room, one thing became clear: we needed an approach in which information would not become the enemy.

This was a critical internal STOP that helped us all focus on not inserting our ideas and interpretations into the information. Suddenly, the information was just that: information—important and serious, but simply information that the client deserved to know. That made it much easier to present the information in a nonconfrontational way.

As we presented the survey responses, it became clear that the group needed HELP to interpret statements. First, we used STOP to slow down the flow of information so that it wasn't overwhelming. One concept at a time, we discussed and clarified what the results meant. Each time a reaction began to surface, we consciously did an internal STOP and remained neutral; then did a STOP on the client as well. Second, we requested the client's HELP in understanding what the results meant. Third, we put ASK into the mix; we asked questions and supported those attending the session when they asked questions of others in the group.

Using STOP, HELP, and ASK at each point allowed all of us to be more objective and less emotional. The group could digest this unsettling information in a collaborative, brainstorming manner and express their thoughts about it. Without feeling attacked by what they were hearing, they could begin to assimilate the insights and build on them.

One person stepped forward and said, "You seem to be saying that we don't adhere to our core beliefs." We responded: "Core beliefs? Sorry, a little HELP. Are you saying that these are our interpretations?" She said, "Yes, of course." We replied, "We're sorry if that's your impression, but this material is directly related to your team's responses and not ours. Would you like to talk more about that?" She said, "No, but, I guess I'm realizing we need to appreciate each other more."

It was a breakthrough. The S.H.A.R.E.™ Tools had allowed her to feel safe enough to take the RISK of delivering the difficult message she was gleaning from the survey results.

With that observation, true dialogue began. Everyone opened up. We began to EXPLORE ways to resolve roadblocks to this company's success.

It worked. They crafted a plan based on an idea we developed that involved everyone in the business. This took on a life of its own. In eighteen months, revenues doubled. In addition, plans for a new computer system that had been lumbering along came together and the implementation was a success. Two family members who had been at each other's throats became friends again.

It was a great success that added value to the business and to personal relationships within the family. To begin to accomplish all of this, we had to be able to STOP reactions to misunderstandings. STOP was the start of something remarkable for this business.

STOP Chapter Key Concepts

- STOP can be gracious when used to create better understanding.

- STOP can be used to STOP ourselves and others.

- STOP can be used anytime in a conversation to protect ourselves or others.

Adding Value with STOP

- When we STOP for clarification, the value is more efficient communication and work flow.

• When we STOP run-on speakers, the value is saving time and getting back on point to advance the process.

• When we STOP ourselves, the value is bringing everyone back into the conversation to create more powerful results together.

Action Steps

In your conversations during the next week, try:

• STOP three times for understanding with someone else

• STOP three times for yourself

For example, you might find opportunities to STOP for understanding when:

• You're being given instructions or directions you don't clearly understand

• You're in a meeting and the speaker is using unfamiliar acronyms or terms

• You're getting confused when someone is telling you something that happened

You might STOP yourself when:

• You're giving instructions and find yourself talking for several minutes

• You're having a reaction, emotional or otherwise, to something someone is telling you

• You're talking over your coworkers or friends and not giving them a chance to participate

Your Observations

- What happened in conversations when you requested that someone STOP?

- What made it easy or difficult for you to request that someone STOP?

- Did you learn new ways to do a gracious STOP?

- What happened when you did STOP yourself?

- How did you add value by using STOP?

Our Observations

It seems as if it would be simple to request someone to STOP, particularly if your purpose is to understand, but we've found that STOP can be the most difficult of the S.H.A.R.E.™ Tools. Here are reasons it may feel difficult to STOP:

- Many have been trained that interrupting is not polite behavior. The gracious STOP lets you take responsibility for understanding information or situations so you can respond or participate appropriately.

- If we have to STOP the speaker because we don't understand, we might think we'll look stupid. Think of how much worse it might look if you try to act on information that you don't fully understand.

- We worry that our interruption will be considered a power play. Only you know whether you're attempting to gain power or trying to understand. If your genuine purpose is to get a better understanding of ideas, situations, or information, your STOP will be accepted in the spirit in which it is given.

- We don't want the speaker to know or to think that we've tuned out. Though it might be uncomfortable, it's better to admit that you "momentarily lost focus" or "briefly got distracted" and need to get back up to speed than risk having your lack of understanding exposed at a later time.

There is strength and power in using the S.H.A.R.E.™ Tools. Using STOP adds value for everyone:

- When you STOP the speaker for clarification, you're supporting that speaker in becoming more accountable for what he means.

- When you STOP and ASK the speaker to clarify what she means, you may also be opening the speaker's mind to other ideas and options.

- When you use STOP with a run-on speaker (yourself or someone else), you take responsibility for getting the conversation back on track.

- When you use STOP when under attack, you demonstrate strength. You are finding a way to protect yourself while continuing to work toward reaching a common ground.

A single STOP can revolutionize the whole conversation. Remember Mary, who found a way to STOP her boss when he was yelling about a client? By using STOP to protect herself from his anger, she changed the dynamic of their relationship and became a recognized contributor in her firm. It may not happen overnight—change takes time—but change can begin when you start with STOP.

CHAPTER 3

HELP—THE WORD THAT EMPOWERS US ALL

HELP is the glue of the S.H.A.R.E.™ Tools. While STOP can position us for success, HELP forges connections, enabling people to work together to resolve, solve, invent, and create new ideas and new environments for success.

How many conversations do you hear where people are talking at each other, not with each other? It's as if they're struggling to be heard, instead of taking a moment to STOP and realize that embracing HELP might be the next step. It's like not asking for directions when we're lost. Significant time and energy can be saved when we admit we're lost and ask for HELP to move forward with everyone more on the same page.

Recently Mark was discussing two paragraphs in a merger agreement with a client's attorney. It was clear that Mark and the client's attorney thought differently about these paragraphs, and Mark found himself defending a position. He quickly realized the conversation was headed downhill: He wasn't saying what he wanted to say, he wasn't listening as well as he should, they were not on the same page, and he was struggling to make himself understood.

He said, "Harriet, I need some HELP. Could we STOP and start this over? I'm realizing that I need to understand more before I can comment on the paragraphs. Can we do that?" She agreed, and they started to HELP each other understand the wording of these paragraphs. In doing so, they discovered that the wording was confusing and wasn't what either of them wanted. If they hadn't identified this issue, the agreement would have been circulated to the other ten people involved and caused an even bigger misunderstanding.

This was a prime example of how success doesn't come from what we know, but from what we need to know. Clarifying and solving this issue saved time, maximized energy and brain power, enhanced understanding, and saved a lot of money. A huge additional benefit: it created a sense of trust that Mark and Harriet could work together to make this agreement really successful.

HELP creates a space where we can find out what's really happening, discover others' perceptions, and allow new ideas to bloom instead of being crushed.

Actually using the word "help" is essential in making HELP most effective. For example, compare these approaches:

- "I can't understand you." versus "I'm trying to understand but going nowhere; can you HELP?"

- "Tell me what you mean." versus "I'm trying to get my head around this idea, but I can't get it. Would you HELP?"

- "What do you mean by that?" versus "Can you HELP me with that idea?"

The first phrases can imply that the speaker is at fault and unable to express ideas to the satisfaction of the listener. But when the listener says, "Can you HELP?" the listener is taking responsibility for his or her own understanding. This is how HELP changes attitudes and invites collaboration.

The *Merriam-Webster Dictionary* defines "help" as having multiple meanings:

1. to give or provide what is necessary to accomplish a task or satisfy a need; contribute strength or means to; render assistance to; cooperate effectively with; aid; assist

2. to save; rescue; succor

3. to make easier or less difficult; contribute to; facilitate.

Here's how HELP accomplishes all of these aims.

HELP to Get Things Done and Add Value

When you request HELP, you're saying, "I want us to move forward positively by being sure we are clear." HELP does its magic by establishing a safety net for everyone in the conversation. With a safe environment in place, people can begin to ASK their questions and begin to build understanding and cooperation. If you find you can't establish an atmosphere of HELP, go back to STOP. If you request HELP again and still can't establish it, you may need to exit instead of trying to make it work at this time. Without an atmosphere of cooperation, how can there be a productive conversation?

Here's an example of how HELP works to get things done:

You: "Bill, may we STOP for a minute? I'm a bit confused. Could you HELP . . . ?"

Bill: "Sure, but would it work if I said it again a different way?"

You: "Okay, shoot."

Bill then describes the situation again.

You: "That helps, thanks, but I realize there are three things I'd like to find out more about—could you HELP again?"

Bill: "What are they?"

Now you're off and running.

When you use HELP, you add value for yourself by reaching a better understanding of what's being said. You add value for others by offering them the opportunity to clarify ideas. Long-term value is added because everyone can move forward with a more solid foundation.

HELP can be especially powerful in sales, when you definitely want to move the conversation forward, but at the customer's/client's pace. HELP makes sure you have the qualified prospect at the right time for the appropriate products/services.

For instance, suppose you're talking with a potential customer and you feel things are going well—until you realize that they're describing their machines differently than in your first meeting. You say, "Al, could we STOP a minute to HELP me get clear on something?" "Sure," Al replies. You say, "When we talked last week, I understood that the Ultra machines are your primary manufacturing line. Then today in the group meeting, I heard that the Spectra machines are your core production products. Could you clarify, please?" You have established a point where you can work together to determine real customer need. If Al says, "Good point; I can see how that can be confusing. What I mean is. . . ." you and Al are on your way together.

HELP to the Rescue

HELP can come to our rescue in challenging situations. You can HELP advance a contentious conversation, clear the air about sensitive subjects, and get everyone back on track when disagreement sets in. Just as there's an internal STOP, there's an internal HELP to rescue us when we realize that we're going down the wrong path (for example, "I'm going to lose this sale"). Or we may engage HELP to rescue the speaker, who may be unclear, moving off point, losing the audience's attention, or creating ill will among the listeners.

STOP and HELP together can be used when we need to exit a conversation that's careened off track. When emotions and distractions run high, using STOP alone to exit might seem abrupt and cause problems. When you request HELP, it can defuse the intensity of the conversation and give everyone a chance to hit reset and get on the same page.

A business contact of ours used HELP to salvage a situation for himself and a vendor. He had placed an order for some materials he needed for a project, providing a post office box address for the shipment. Instead, the vendor sent the materials to a street address. Our colleague had several conversations with the post office and the vendor, trying to locate the materials. The package was returned to the vendor. Then, a customer service representative for the vendor called to follow up. Ordinarily, this call would be meant to mend fences. This was not that kind of call.

The customer service representative had a list of questions. Without the benefit of the S.H.A.R.E.™ Tools, those questions seemed combative and laden with blame for our colleague about the shipping problems. As he recalled what happened, he said, "I had to use STOP on myself because I was getting angry, but I needed her HELP to fix the problem. In using STOP for myself, I realized that she needed my input to understand what had happened with the package, but her questions were so accusatory that they weren't resolving the problem.

"I let HELP take the lead and kept thinking, 'How can I HELP her HELP me?' As I used the word 'help' more in the conversation, her tone changed. I said, 'Could you HELP me help us to better understand?' 'I guess,' she said. I said, 'I'd like to ASK a few questions to make sure I understand everything you are saying; would that work?'

She said, 'Okay.' That certainly worked better than telling her what they had done wrong with shipping. It took time, but I was able to get everything cleared up and the package got shipped to my correct mailing address. HELP was the most important Tool in taking this conversation from argumentative to productive. And keeping anger out of the conversation improved the day for both of us."

This Revolutionary Conversation™ is a great example of how we can use the Tools to come alongside others—even those who seem to be causing the problems. Coming alongside adds value and increases effectiveness. It shouldn't be confused with rolling over or giving in. It just means that instead of "my idea/your idea," we're going to see how our ideas fit into the puzzle and co-create a better solution.

HELP Makes Things Easier

Consider how you would respond to the following statements:

- "Tell me what you mean."
- "Could you HELP me understand what you mean?"

The first sentence is more demanding and might back the speaker into a corner. The second creates a collaborative feeling. The very word HELP creates its own particular magic and willingness to help.

Recently, Barbara needed to transfer money between business accounts. She couldn't go to the bank, and her phone calls weren't being returned. She e-mailed her favorite teller and requested his HELP to get this transaction completed. HELP was in the subject line of that e-mail. In less than a minute, she had a response that made the transfer possible immediately. She told us that the real difference was in requesting assistance and using the word "help" with the right person. Up to that point, she had tried to call, leave a message to tell them what she wanted. To get to HELP, she had to realize that when things don't work, it may be time to STOP what we're doing and change the pattern instead of continuing to force a situation that was going nowhere.

Alternatively, Barbara could have called the teller for HELP and said, "I can't understand what to do next. Can you HELP me sort this out?" He might have replied, "Sure, what can I do?" Barbara could then ASK, "Could you describe how this is different from the other times I've moved money? Has something changed that I might not know about?" By using HELP–ASK, she could have learned what was necessary to get her money transferred.

STOP–HELP to Save Time

Everyone is extremely busy—too much to do and never enough time. STOP–HELP has become a real time-saver for a service provider of ours, one who is running her own business from home while caring for her young children.

"I get a lot of inquiry calls from all over the world from people seeking information. The calls aren't about my services, and they take so much time. I have to answer these calls, but it was really adding to my stress level because the callers were taking so long to get to the point and pulling me away from work I have to do.

"One day, after taking a S.H.A.R.E.® Workshop, it dawned on me that I could use STOP–HELP to move these calls forward in a constructive way. I tried it on the first call. I knew the caller needed my HELP—my attitude had changed.

"First, I needed to know the purpose of her call. After requesting that she STOP for a moment, I said that I needed HELP to understand what she wanted. I began to ASK questions that allowed me to understand what she wanted more quickly. I stopped trying to save the situation by having all the answers and opted to find out what was happening instead.

"I now use S.H.A.R.E.™ Tools in all my calls. When appropriate, we move into RISK and EXPLORE, which helps find solutions that meet everyone's needs. The Tools have saved me hours of time, not to mention the aggravation I was causing myself. Although each call is different, my basic approach goes like this:

'Eileen, could we slow down a minute? You're providing a lot of good information. Could you HELP me understand your situation? If I could ASK you some questions, maybe we could get a better sense of how I might HELP.' "

She found that this time-saver turned out to be a moneymaker, too, increasing her billable hours and converting more inquiries into paying clients. And she worked more efficiently, so she could spend more time with her family. It was a win-win all around!

Giving and Receiving HELP

HELP is a two-way street. You can benefit by receiving and giving HELP. Let's look at an example of how this can work. Phil, an entrepreneur and a successful business owner, has received a bill from Ralph, his CPA. He is not happy with the charges and immediately calls Ralph.

"Listen, Ralph," Phil begins, "I got this bill for five thousand dollars. I had no idea this project would be so expensive. What's going on?"

Ralph is speechless. For one thing, he hears the anger in Phil's voice and knows he's got a very annoyed client on his hands. For another, try as he might, he has no recollection of performing services that would have led to such a large bill.

Ralph first needs to catch his breath, STOP himself from reacting, and switch gears into collaborative HELP mode: "Phil, I need a moment to catch up. I'm both curious and surprised, but I'd like to know more. Can you HELP me get up to speed?"

Phil says, "It's simple. The fee is too high."

Ralph, knowing he has to keep his head in order to retain his client, calmly returns to STOP and HELP to try and understand the situation better and advance the conversation in a positive way: "Phil, in order to HELP, I need to understand what happened. Do you think you could HELP me figure out the facts of the situation?"

Phil: "Okay, but I don't have much time. What do you need to know?"

Ralph can continue to use STOP and HELP until he understands why they had different expectations of what the fee would be. Phil can gain a better understanding of what services were provided and the value he receives.

As it turned out, Ralph and Phil had initially discussed a smaller fee for a specific service with finite parameters. After their agreement, Phil called Ralph's associate for additional analysis. The associate assumed that his boss, Ralph, knew about the call and went ahead and did the work the client wanted. Phil assumed that the associate had cleared the work with Ralph and that the service fell under the original pricing. So Phil, expecting the original amount on the bill, was unpleasantly surprised that it was so much higher. Ralph hadn't even known about the additional work and increased amount and was blindsided by Phil's angry call. Once everything was uncovered, Phil paid his bill based on the new understanding.

Another way to approach this caller could be to use a Complete STOP: "Phil, could we STOP a minute? It would really HELP me if I could do some quick research to find out what happened. Can I call you later?"

Either way, using the word HELP creates the opportunity for "we" instead of "you" versus "me." In business and in life, relationships are our most valuable assets. HELP lets you preserve and develop those precious assets.

Sometimes, requesting HELP is more subtle, but it's there none-theless.

Noal was working with a business to develop its new human resources department. Someone was needed to handle day-to-day activities with Noal's oversight. The client's senior management wanted Sam, a favorite of the owner, to assume this role, even though he had no HR experience. Noal describes the transition:

"When Sam and I first started talking about HR duties, I found myself going on and on about regulations and requirements as if I were talking to a colleague who had the same basic knowledge as I did. Sam, without having any training in the S.H.A.R.E.™ Tools, intuitively knew what to do with me. He said, 'I'm confused!' After a few of those comments, as I was driving home, I realized that I needed to use the S.H.A.R.E.™ Tools to STOP myself and HELP Sam. I didn't want to talk down to him. He was bright and quick, but he had no frame of reference to understand the HR language I was speaking.

"In our subsequent meetings, I consciously began to STOP myself and request HELP to be sure I was making sense. It wasn't about asking him if he understood. It was about asking myself whether I'd said it clearly. I'd STOP and seek HELP for myself and ASK: 'Am I really helping? Could I be clearer? Could I come up with a better example?' I also looked to Sam for HELP by having him relay what he thought I was saying. In addition, I asked him if he would HELP me by giving me some pointers. We were both learning.

"After working with Sam for a while, he began to pick up the Tools without any formal instruction. Just by using them together, we enhanced our conversational skills. Over time, Sam developed into an effective HR manager, able to talk with vendors and employees to get the information that was needed.

"When I look back and think how it might have gone without the Tools, I can see how Sam could have become frustrated with my long-winded explanations, possibly deciding that HR was not for him. It would have been a loss for that business and for the profession. Even with only one of us actively using the S.H.A.R.E.™ Tools, we were able to bridge knowledge and experience gaps. The Tools became even more powerful with both of us using them. 'I'm confused' remains part of our communication pattern. Either of us can say it, and often the other responds, 'Me, too!' With a laugh, we can regroup and figure it out together."

Noal's experience demonstrates how HELP can be contagious! By establishing an atmosphere of helping each other, they created an environment of learning and engagement:

> • Noal became more effective and intuitive at training others.

> • Sam could better understand unfamiliar information, expand his knowledge of the technical aspects of his position, and contribute more to the company.

> • Sam improved his self-esteem by being more comfortable requesting HELP.

> • Most important, Noal and Sam together created a stronger HR department.

HELP-aphobia?

There's a "help" button on every website, on our computer desktop, and on our iPhones. We don't have trouble using HELP there, but when it comes to conversation, often it's a different story. Requesting HELP sounds simple, yet we often resist doing it. Some think that seeking HELP is a sign of weakness. In fact, it's a sign of strength and commitment. With HELP, we're letting others know that we're committed to understanding what they're saying, actively involved in the conversation, and open to learning.

When we genuinely seek HELP, people almost always come to our aid. But after years of using the S.H.A.R.E.™ Tools, we've seen how difficult it can be for some people to seek HELP. We've also seen how, once they can get past whatever is holding them back and give HELP a chance, they often feel a great sense of relief.

A colleague was extremely reluctant to ask for HELP. She'd spend hours trying to figure out how to do something in a software program rather than say, "I need HELP to understand this." But after using HELP a few times, she began to trust that requesting assistance put her in a stronger position than if she struggled to figure it out on her own: "I never realized how heavy the burden of not seeking HELP was. Once I started requesting HELP in all kinds of conversations, it freed me up to focus on what mattered. Now, I'm seeking HELP everywhere. I find that I get everything done in half the time. I never realized how much time I wasted trying to figure things out alone. I delegate more and seek out people to work on projects. I would have never done this in the past." She revitalized her life by not having to always have the answer but instead being open to new information and ideas.

S.H.A.R.E.™ Tools in Action

How Looking for HELP from Customers
Grew a Business Tenfold

The owners of a small distributorship wanted to grow their business rapidly but had no clue how to do it. Mark worked with them on a number of areas: setting up a customer service-driven computer system, purchasing another business, developing a more sophisticated sales force. These efforts were all effective, but they paled in comparison to the work we did with their customers.

It was clear that the business was securing a larger-than-normal gross profit per product and per customer, but it was unclear why. They had high-quality sales professionals who were doing well; they were paid commissions as a percentage of gross profit. However, it was unclear why the sales professionals were so successful.

Together, Mark and the owners decided to interview customers to understand why they were responding so well to these products and their services. They picked several diverse businesses to interview and developed a customized questionnaire to use as a guide in the interviews. The goal was to discover how this business had been able to charge their customers more than their competition. The sales director, who was an owner, and Mark met with customers for interviews where HELP was the focus.

The first few customer meetings were interesting but rather bland and unenlightening. The sixth customer said he liked the products and thought the salespeople were good; nothing unique was mentioned. The big question was still why this customer was willing to pay more than he would to other distributors.

As Mark and the sales director left the interview, the customer's purchasing agent came running up, wanting help. He had drawings for them to deliver to the company's research and development (R&D) department. The sales director and Mark looked at each other. What they knew, but this customer obviously didn't, was that there was no R&D department! They definitely needed HELP to understand what was going on. Mark turned back to the purchasing agent and said, "Can we go over these with you to HELP us clearly understand the drawings?" He agreed.

They talked with the purchasing agent about the drawings, while indirectly trying to understand how, apparently, customers thought there was an R&D department. They needed HELP to get their questions answered without appearing ignorant and without his feeling that they were interrogating him.

It worked. By the time they walked out the door, they had discovered that, unbeknownst to the owners and management, the salespeople had found a way to HELP produce new and improved products for their customers and had secured more business through this value-added approach!

Back at the plant, they discovered that there was a makeshift R&D process in which sales professionals and a plant supervisor were working with these plans and drawings to assist customers in developing better ways to manufacture products.

With this new information, Mark and the sales director interviewed other customers, including questions about R&D and how they liked the results. Everyone liked the results they were receiving from R&D.

So, what did the company do? Thanks to the information HELP uncovered, they created a formal R&D department. Over the next five years, the business's revenues grew tenfold. HELP paid off in a big way.

HELP Chapter Key Concepts

- HELP creates a more gracious STOP.

- Requesting HELP creates an opportunity for collaboration and understanding.

- By requesting HELP, we advance the conversation.

- With HELP, we demonstrate a willingness to receive assistance.

• The word "help" itself has the power to turn around a conversation for all participants.

• Within the mutually supportive context of HELP, questions become collaborative, not interrogative.

Adding Value with HELP

When you request HELP, you add value by empowering everyone in the conversation to participate in collaboration.

• Everyone has more information and clarity.

• You can find ways to engage or reengage in the conversation.

• The speaker has an opportunity to make sure his message is understood.

• Others feel comfortable and safe in participating.

• A bond can be created between participants.

Action Steps—STOP and HELP Together

In practicing STOP, you've probably already started to integrate HELP into conversations. As you continue to use STOP and HELP, you may find that:

• People respond more openly because you've let them know you're not trying to dominate the conversation.

• You're more comfortable taking responsibility for your own ideas and thoughts.

• STOP demonstrates that you're not shy but empowered, and HELP indicates your willingness to learn and engage.

• STOP–HELP is gracious but also communicates that you want to move forward and advance the process.

With this in mind, identify daily at least:

• Three new situations where you might STOP yourself to request HELP

• Three new situations where you might STOP others to seek HELP

Examples of times to STOP yourself and request HELP:

• When you're beginning to disagree with what someone is saying

• When you realize that you've gone off on a tangent

• When you see that the person you're talking with may not understand

Examples where you might STOP others to request HELP:

• With a coworker who is upset about something that happened in the office

• When the speaker is rambling and/or presenting conflicting information

• When something has happened and the group is becoming frustrated, restless, or angry

Your Observations

• How did your requesting HELP affect the other person?

• How did you feel about requesting HELP?

• What was the impact of requesting HELP on the outcome of the conversation?

- How did you add value by using **HELP**?

- What were some of the triggers or indicators that motivated you to **STOP** and request **HELP**?

Our Observations

Words matter. When we think of great speeches or lines of poetry, we become aware of how important words can be. The words "I have a dream" by Dr. Martin Luther King Jr. have resonated for decades. John F. Kennedy's words, "Ask not what your country can do for you—ask what you can do for your country," changed the course of a nation. These are public words designed to stir a profound response in listeners. But many everyday words can make a significant difference in how our conversations and relationships work. We've experienced countless times how using the word HELP can defuse anger, bring people together, create an atmosphere for collaboration, and change the dynamic of conversations. HELP is one of the most powerful words, and when combined with the rest of the Tools, it can revolutionize your ability to add value and for others to add value to you.

As you practice HELP, give the words below a try and see how your conversations change. It can be fun and you'll be pleasantly surprised at what can happen along the way!

Please and Thank You

"Please" and "thank you" are gracious ways to acknowledge someone's work, participation, contribution, ideas, and feelings, even when you disagree. They can make a difference in people's willingness to engage in conversations. Acknowledging how others have helped you can go a long way toward creating a long-term association or relationship.

I versus We

Conversations dominated by "I" are closed conversations. The S.H.A.R.E.™ Tools encourage participation and dialogue, which keeps information flowing. Using the word "we" changes the whole feeling of the conversation. You'll notice that we use the word "we" often in this book. We use it in our consulting work, too, because our goal is to join with our clients so that we all can accomplish something remarkable. Using the word "we" with the S.H.A.R.E.™ Tools reinforces the sense of partnership and collaboration.

This does not mean to never say I. "I have a question," "I am confused," or "I am thinking that we might get some HELP from our team leader" and the like are all perfectly appropriate. You're taking responsibility, not taking over. That will HELP collaboration flourish.

A final word about HELP—and a friendly warning. When the HELP you've requested of another is given, it's a gift not to be squandered or abused. If you ask for HELP and then turn it around to take control of the conversation, you may never get the chance to ask for HELP again from those you were working with. Use HELP wisely and it will reward you with many Revolutionary Conversations™.

CHAPTER 4

ASK—THE KEY TO UNDERSTANDING

A SK expands the foundation for understanding and success. It is the place where all parties can begin to appreciate the situation and its nuances. By requesting additional information, clarifying key points, honoring others' perceptions, and building a bridge to agreement, we can advance the process or discussion, develop concepts and ideas, get work done, resolve issues, or deepen a relationship.

Of course, we've all asked questions during conversations. What's revolutionary about ASK is that when it's preceded by HELP, it removes the perception of interrogation, criticism, doubt, or blame and creates a more collaborative and robust environment where people can be more comfortable engaging and disclosing. It's not so much "What can I learn," but "What can we learn together?" HELP–ASK fosters what we like to call coming alongside and makes Q&A a joint effort.

A Closer Look at Questions

To maximize the benefit of ASK, let's look at how questions work.

Open and Closed

You can ASK questions in different ways. You could say, "You don't want to buy this insurance policy, do you?" Guess what the answer will likely be? A closed-ended question puts the listener in the position of being able to answer only "Yes" or "No." Or you could use the S.H.A.R.E.™ Tools and ASK, "If I am to assist you, I need your HELP to understand what you want to accomplish with insurance. Is this a good time to ask some questions? Could you tell me about your plans for retirement?" The answer could be anything from owning a scuba diving company in Australia to becoming a hermit in Antarctica. But until you have that information, you have no way of knowing how to proceed. That's the beauty of an open-ended question: it encourages the speaker to elaborate. Consider these ideas for open-ended questions:

> • "Could you tell me more about what you mean when you say 'profit participation'?"
>
> • "I'm unfamiliar with the terms 'organizational alignment' and 'employee engagement.' Could you explain those to me?"
>
> • "Can you give me an example of a time when you had to resolve a conflict between two employees?"

Closed-ended questions ("Where have you been? Why? Why didn't you go somewhere else?") may be great for busy environments or for questioning a witness during a trial. While they can bring specific information to light because of their strong focus, they limit responses, which can end conversations. The S.H.A.R.E.™ Tools use open-ended questions to keep conversation going and make it possible to engage in dialogue, encourage the speaker to expand on ideas, and (with STOP–HELP) give the listener multiple chances to understand and ensure that important information is not missed.

It's essential that ASK not be a one-sided endeavor. All the parties can use ASK again and again until everyone understands each other clearly.

Collaborative

Collaborative questions are questions "we" are ASKing together. They challenge us to think more deeply about a situation or an issue. For example:

- "What do we need to learn about this subject/this situation?"

- "What do we need to find out in order to take action on this?"

- "What questions should we be asking about this?"

- "How do we use this information to everyone's advantage?"

Collaborative questions elevate the discussion and encourage everyone's input. They can be especially powerful in times of change, drama, or operational or cultural shift.

As we've worked with clients and the S.H.A.R.E™ Tools, we've included collaborative questions more and more in our group conversations. We find they go beyond just soliciting more information and allow conversations to build and gain dimension.

Using STOP–HELP–ASK to Get Things Done

Demands on our time and pressure to produce results have many of us stretched to the limit, and many of us feel we're being buried in information. The S.H.A.R.E.™ Tools let you zero in on the information you need in order to be more effective.

Are You the Right Employee for Us?

Finding the right candidate for a job entails a significant investment of time and energy. Using the S.H.A.R.E.™ Tools can help create an interview environment that encourages dialogue and puts you and the candidate more at ease, enabling both of you to determine whether this is the right fit. STOP, HELP, and ASK can support discovering details of a candidate's experience, soft skills, and attitudes. By hiring well, you add value by reducing the cost of turnover and creating strong, compatible work groups. Consider this example:

Joanne, HR manager at a small, growing business, is looking to fill the office manager position. She wants someone who can grow with the business. The perfect candidate would be highly organized and able to supervise people and maintain a positive attitude while handling multiple priorities in a fast-paced environment. Joanne reviews a number of résumés and decides to interview Emma, whose résumé indicates she has the skill set and experience that Joanne is looking for to fill the position.

During the interview, Joanne asks Emma to discuss her role as office manager at her previous employer. Emma tells her that she did "everything." Rather than respond, "That's good, because someone who can do everything here would be a dream come true," Joanne follows up with, " 'Everything' is quite a lot [STOP]. Can you HELP me understand what 'everything' meant at that company? Could you give me some examples of your daily responsibilities? [ASK an open-ended question.]"

Emma lists a few tasks and, when she brings up supervision, Joanne says, "Supervision can be challenging [STOP]. Everyone has a different style. Could you clarify [HELP] by giving me an example of a time you needed to address an employee problem? [ASK an open-ended question.]"

Emma starts to talk about a problem with the company's receptionist: "She always came in late. I told her that she needed to be on time every day. You have to nip these things in the bud."

Joanne might say, "'To nip things in the bud' is an interesting expression. To be sure I understand, could you tell me more about what that means to you?"

"Well," Emma replies, "that means that I told her being late could not be a habit. Right away, I put her on notice about being on time!"

Joanne continues, "I understand it's a problem when someone is late. I'm curious. How did you discover what was causing her to be late?"

The conversation goes forward with Joanne continuing to use STOP–HELP–ASK to reveal more about Emma's general skills, interpersonal communication skills, and supervisory style. Using open-ended questions keeps Emma engaged in the conversation, expanding on ideas and providing more details. Whether or not Joanne decides that Emma is the right candidate, by using the S.H.A.R.E.™ Tools and open-ended questions, she will have a much better understanding of Emma's skills and how she might fit into the organization.

What makes this a Revolutionary Conversation™ is that both people engage in a conversation, not an interrogation; when you just shoot questions and answers back and forth in an interview, the pieces often don't add up. STOP–HELP–ASK changes that by building a coherent, dimensional body of information. The more the employer and the candidate learn about each other, the better the chances are that you both can make good decisions in the hiring process. That adds up to more engaged employees and a lower turnover rate—two factors that contribute significantly to the bottom line.

Are You the Right Employer for Me?

The S.H.A.R.E.™ Tools can be very useful for a candidate, too, to find out as much as possible about a prospective employer. Using STOP–HELP–ASK, you can get a clear understanding of job expectations, workplace culture, and potential for advancement. Open-ended questions give you the opportunity to see beyond the job description into the reality of the workplace. You may also find ways to demonstrate how hiring you would add value to the business. Here's an example of this process in action:

Gerald has been looking for a job for several months and has recently found an opportunity he feels hopeful about. His biggest issue is keeping his enthusiasm in check so that he doesn't just sign on to a new position without making sure everything is as good as it seems. But he's also worried that asking too many questions could put off his future employer. This is where STOP–HELP–ASK comes in handy to both demonstrate interest and learn more about the position and company.

Gerald is meeting with his potential new boss. Everything is going well until he hears that he may need to travel out of the country. His thoughts take off on that tangent and he realizes he needs an internal STOP, saying to himself, I need some HELP. I want this job, but I need to find out what's expected regarding travel.

Gerald says, "Mr. Rose, could we STOP a moment? I'm a bit confused. Could we talk about travel for this position [HELP]?"

"Of course," Mr. Rose replies. "What do you need to know?"

"I didn't know travel was involved, so let me understand," Gerald continues. "Did I hear you correctly that there will be international travel?"

Mr. Rose explains, "About twice a year; we visit all of the company facilities in Europe, which takes about two weeks. You'll be traveling with our general manager, Mr. Burke."

Gerald says, "It sounds like a lot of travel, even though it's only twice a year. I've traveled in the U.S. but I'm new to international travel. Could you HELP me understand more about the differences

[ASK an open-ended question], and the kind of work we would do on these trips? [ASK a collaborative question.]"

The conversation continues as questions are asked and answered about the duties of the trip, the accommodations, how the travelers stay in touch with their families and with the office, and other topics. This allows Gerald to come alongside a concept that he was tentative about. Finally he stops and says, "It sounds like an interesting opportunity to learn what's really happening at the other offices, strengthen my connections with the overseas teams, and return with a fresh perspective. That sounds exciting. Thank you."

If Gerald hadn't used STOP–HELP–ASK to learn more about the travel for the position, he might have left the interview feeling this job was not for him. If Mr. Rose had mentally crossed Gerald off the list as soon as he realized Gerald hadn't traveled overseas, he might have lost a valuable future employee. When they both took the time to interact and explain, Gerald became even more excited about the position, and both he and Mr. Rose had a better interview. What made this a Revolutionary Conversation™ is that Gerald avoided "selling himself" or "being sold." The S.H.A.R.E.™ Tools created a bridge to a hiring decision based in reality.

What Do We Need in Order to Accomplish This?

A manufacturing business that was struggling to implement its operational plan invited us to work with them. They needed to streamline the process between the time an order was placed and the time it was shipped. They had purchased a sophisticated software program that promised to do everything they thought they needed and more. They had spent large sums of money on consultants and trainers trying to get this system up and running. In the meantime, they were alienating their customers because turnaround was getting longer, not shorter.

First, we did STOP to prevent ourselves and our client from repeating the same mistakes they'd experienced in the past and started looking for HELP from people on the line. We began to ASK questions at the user level. We interviewed everyone who used the technology, from the inside sales team to the crews on the loading dock. We wanted to understand their needs and how the system worked for them in real time.

The more questions we asked, the clearer it became that the technology wasn't working at the user level. The project was stalled because the company had not created an environment of HELP where everyone had an opportunity to contribute and ASK questions for additional information.

Once we had gathered and shared the information, we worked with the software designers to make changes in the software to meet the needs of the company and this industry. By reaching out to everyone in the business to understand their needs and perceptions, we were able to design a more appropriate system that got more support from the users. It became "their" system—which made for a better environment all around. They were open to working with the changes and with us to assess the viability of the new system, including testing the changes as they became available. This process involved everyone, which created a bond throughout the company and made the new system work. An important aspect here was the use of the collaborative question, which helped everyone to feel that they weren't just part of the question, but also part of the answer.

With the new order process in place, delivery time decreased by 35%. Customers were happier. Business was increasing. Word got around about the company's superior fulfillment process, and new customers began to seek them out as a preferred provider. Thanks to ASK, everyone won!

As you seek to improve your organization by adopting new procedures or technologies, the more information you can gather early in the development process about the nature of the situation the better. Trying to solve a problem or create a whole new way to operate without information from everyone involved is like trying to assemble a jigsaw puzzle without turning over all the pieces. It's a perfect example of success coming not from what you know, but from what you need to know. It takes time in the beginning but saves countless hours and money in the long run. ASK is essential in that process. This one experience for the company helped them to see that reaching out in a collaborative way could enhance their whole process of creating new ideas and new products.

Do We Need Another Meeting?

A major complaint we hear is that meetings take too long and never accomplish anything. We've all been in meetings that were boring, confusing, or combative. What if, at the end of a meeting, you had advanced the process and had a clear direction for what happens next? Sound impossible? Not with STOP–HELP–ASK. We'll show you how.

Jake, vice president of marketing for an ad agency, is starting his weekly status meeting with his team. As a "big picture" person, he always sees the vision of the completed project flashing on the jumbo screen of life. He's known for being quite the orator and holds the unofficial company record for longest presentations without interruption. Everybody likes Jake—and clients love him—but when his staff leaves his meetings, they often scramble to put the pieces together.

Jake's team—Irene, the production manager; Albert, the graphic designer; Rachel, the IT manager—have just finished a S.H.A.R.E.®

class and have agreed to work together to try out the new skills they've learned. They're determined that this meeting will be meaningful for everyone attending and that they will stick to the agenda as well as keep their eyes and ears open for ways each can add more value to the meeting.

Jake begins by talking about the projects in production. Before long, he becomes excited by his vision of how these projects will earn industry awards for best ad campaign.

Irene says, "Jake, I see your excitement. I'm excited, too. Could we slow down for a minute? I'm lost; where are we on the agenda?"

Jake identifies the spot and Irene asks one more question to better understand what is being done.

They continue the discussion, back on track with their agenda. In a few minutes, Jake digresses into a story about his first ad campaign. This time, Albert uses STOP–HELP–ASK to focus the group on the current agenda item about client feedback and deadlines. They generate some great ideas.

Realizing that Rachel has not had much to say, Irene ASKs, "Rachel, I'm wondering if this could have an impact on your department. Can you HELP us understand how this will all coordinate on the IT side?" With information from Rachel, they can get a clear idea of when and how they can deliver the presentation to the client.

At this point, Albert says, "Let's STOP for a minute before we talk about the next client to be sure we're on the same page and clear about our next steps." They talk about their task lists for that client. Everyone has an opportunity to ASK about his or her role. Albert makes sure that everyone understands the next steps and knows the time line. Jake says, "I'm thinking that a follow-up meeting in three days might be helpful. What do you think?" As this meeting ended, everyone felt it had been one of the best—including Jake, who began to understand how important collaboration can be for successful meetings and that STOP–HELP–ASK contributed to staying on agenda.

What's unique about this interaction is that without taking the meeting away from Jake, his teammates were able to come alongside each other and be sure that all the information got on the table. Everyone took responsibility for their role in the meeting, without taking over. They kept the agenda moving forward, made progress on each project, and ensured that they could be successful all around.

Every meeting is different, depending on its purpose (to deliver information, to generate new ideas, or to solve an existing problem, to name a few); the participants (sometimes, instead of a leader who rambles, we have someone like Andrew in chapter 2, who controls the meeting and eliminates participation); and the business culture. One beauty of the S.H.A.R.E.™ Tools is that they can be used in any setting or business culture to help us leave meetings with more information, a better understanding of a situation, and a clearer idea about what should happen next.

How Jake's team meeting unfolded using S.H.A.R.E.™ also proves that you don't have to lead a meeting to play a leadership role that the organization will value. Both Irene and Albert added value by keeping Jake on point and by clarifying information they all needed. Irene engaged Rachel to be sure the company's technology would support what they wanted to deliver. Encouraging participation from people who may hesitate to speak up is valuable so that we can get all the information we need. Open-ended and collaborative questions can open these doors. Also, we often want to have some direction or resolution at the close of meetings. Meeting productivity can increase exponentially if you ASK clarifying questions at the end to be certain all are on track with their responsibilities, as Albert did. This is especially important in meetings where new concepts and ideas are introduced.

If you're leading a meeting, you can use STOP–HELP–ASK to be sure everyone's on the same page, get all the information on the table, and foster an atmosphere of collaboration leading to agreement, which reinforces forward movement, plans, and action.

What's the Decision?

Remember the troubled family business we told you about in chapter 2? In some companies, people have difficulty communicating with each other, which makes it impossible to reach agreements and make improvements. That company was facing serious competitive challenges in the marketplace, but the combative family dynamic that blocked consensus was an added obstacle. The situation had gotten so bad that the family didn't have a starting place for discussions and couldn't see a possibility of being able to agree on anything.

To save the business, we had to find a way for the ten people in the family management group to be able to interact. When we introduced them to the S.H.A.R.E.™ Tools through a combination of individual coaching and seminars, the family members began to see possibilities for themselves and for their business. To begin, they all adopted the STOP Tool, realizing that they all had to STOP what was going on among themselves if they were to save their business. This Tool alone opened the door to discussions.

We worked with them to establish protocols for conversations using the Tools as a way to begin understanding everyone's perspectives and needs. With STOP–HELP–ASK, they worked through numerous, highly charged family issues; made important decisions for the future of the company; and made sure everyone was heard and every idea considered.

They returned again and again to STOP and HELP—this family's pattern was to engage in free-for-alls with everyone talking over each other. With STOP, they could begin to get some information on the table. In one situation, one of the sisters wanted to ASK a question but couldn't get a word in edgewise. She finally just yelled, "STOP, please. I have a question." That got their attention and she was able to ASK that question.

In the end, our team and the family turned around the company. Working together, we added value by developing a completely new manufacturing process and new ways to work with their customers, branding a new product and increasing revenues by 50%.

Our Revolutionary Conversations™ expanded information and cooperation through direct, open-ended, and many collaborative questions, ensuring that the entire team had all necessary information to move ahead. In the process, the family learned that the negative cost of keeping quiet could be great, and the positive potential of speaking up far outweighed the risk.

Practicing the Art of ASK

Watch any five-year-old and you'll see a master of questions. In their inquisitiveness and desire to learn, children are constantly asking, "Why?" With the Tools we can tap into the natural desire to learn with "What? How? Why?" questions. There are four main characteristics of asking questions with the S.H.A.R.E.™ Tools:

> 1. Open-ended/Collaborative—We've talked about this aspect in previous sections. These questions solicit and uncover additional information, increase everyone's understanding, help the speaker clarify ideas, and engage everyone in the conversation.
>
> 2. Nonconfrontational—Even when not open-ended, questions should not be designed to interrogate or catch someone, as in, "gotcha!"

3. Purposeful—ASK questions move the process forward. You may learn a new piece of information or come to the realization that you have differing points of view. Either way, you've advanced the process. ASK encourages dialogue, not a continuous stream of back-and-forth questions.

4. Thoughtful—The intent of ASK is to add value and enhance the discussion, not to filibuster, curry favor, or cover for lack of attention.

Here are some examples of using ASK to check for understanding:

- "I think I understand how we're going to get trucks there, but I need HELP. What else I should be considering?"

- "I've been presenting a lot of information, and I'm wondering if you might help me outline some questions we can ASK ourselves about what I've said?"

- "I feel like there is something missing . . . can you think of anything else?"

- "Barbara, this is an interesting idea and I think I'm getting it more and more, but could I ASK you two questions about the new software changes for the project?"

What STOP–HELP–ASK Can Accomplish

As you have put STOP–HELP–ASK to work in your conversations, you may have experienced how they flow together in a natural and easy way. There is a rhythm that we can use to help ourselves in any number of situations:

- TO CLARIFY AND DEEPEN A CONVERSATION: "I'm interested in your idea about developing a blog. I need some help to understand how a blog can generate significant presales for product launches. How do you see a blog integrating into our new product introduction?"

• TO STOP YOURSELF DURING A RAMBLE: "I've talked a lot about the September rollout of the ad campaign, and I want to stop here to get your help. What problems or timing issues have we not yet considered in planning this rollout?"

• TO PARAPHRASE FOR UNDERSTANDING: "When we were considering new jelly bean flavors, you mentioned a new grape flavor. I thought we had several grape flavors already. Could you help me understand why we need another?"

You are probably practicing this in your conversations now. One of the joys of the S.H.A.R.E.™ Tools is the continual opportunity to be amazed with what they can do.

During the development of this book, we had an extraordinary experience with STOP–HELP–ASK. Two of us had distinctly different ideas about a chapter subtitle. We each wanted to press our case and persuade everyone else to agree. The tension between us was growing and impacting everyone in the room. One of us is a powerful persuader and can use language to overpower any objections. The other is more likely to acquiesce during conflict, but then withdraw from the situation. With so much at stake, Mark stepped in. He created a group STOP.

What he asked each of us to do was to reenter the discussion using only STOP–HELP–ASK. Neither of us could ramble and both had to participate. The rhythm of STOP–HELP–ASK slowed us down and demanded that we stay present in the conversation instead of thinking about what we would say next to "win" our point. We started face-to-face, still full of the energy we had before. Because we had to stick to only STOP–HELP–ASK, it created an internal STOP for both of us. We had to listen carefully and clarify our thinking before we spoke. As the rhythm fell in place, we engaged each other in a dialogue. We were able to come alongside each other, collaborate, and reach a much better solution than either of us had been promoting before.

There was a sigh of relief in the room when it came together. We still talk about how powerful STOP, HELP, and ASK are and how grateful we are that Mark pulled us back to STOP–HELP–ASK.

What we experienced happens every day in meetings, with teams, and between bosses and employees. When an individual steamrolls others and stops collaboration or someone withdraws from the process, the cost to organizations is enormous. The rhythm of STOP–HELP–ASK has an energy of its own. Whether you use them as an individual or as a global tool to create a collaborative dynamic with groups, they can create revolutionary outcomes. Three little words— so much power.

Got That?

Using STOP–HELP–ASK can be timesavers and stress reducers when giving or receiving instructions.

When you need to give instructions, it's important to explain desired end results. Before you address the team, use STOP–HELP–ASK internally to be clear about what you expect. After you've clearly stated the expected result to the team, you can ASK key questions to be sure everyone is on the same page. To be even more effective, include the opportunity for your team to ask you questions as well. With this kind of collaborative dialogue, you may uncover some issues that had not been anticipated and have an opportunity to solve problems before they arise.

Suppose you're a department head planning a marketing training. You first meet with the office manager, Sally, to start the process. It's a perfect time for STOP-HELP-ASK: "Hi, Sally. I think you heard about the marketing training we'll be doing next month. I was wondering if you could HELP me to organize this event. I haven't done one in a while. Where do you think we should begin?" Sally says, "Well, first, who do we plan to invite? Do you think you might want people from another department to join us?" You say, "To answer your first question, I was thinking of starting small, our twenty-five people only. But inviting other departments is interesting. Can you tell me more?" Sally replies, "Well, I'm thinking that the departments could share the cost, and it might make for some interesting networking and team-building. That make any sense?" You: "Sally, this is getting more interesting. The boss is always talking about the departments never really connecting with each other. This could be a gracious step forward. How do you think we should proceed?" Sally: "Well, I heard about the training in our weekly admin meeting, but I also heard about it from another department—there seems to be interest. If I were you, I would connect with the other three department heads and find out if there is some interest. How does that sound?" You: "Great idea. I will do that this morning."

Then you could continue: "Sally, I'm thinking we might start figuring out the logistics, what do you think?" Sally: "Good idea. How about if I put together a list of action points and questions, and meet with you later this afternoon to discuss?" You: "Okay, but before we break, could we brainstorm about the key items I should highlight in my conversations with the other department heads? I'd like to be really prepared." Sally: "Sure, let's do it right now." And off they go. By using ASK to engage and clarify, you and Sally work together to plan a successful training—one you might never have conceived on your own.

Oops! I Thought That . . . ASK to Avoid Assuming Traps

This conversation may have occurred in your life:

"I thought you were going to pick me up at the airport!"

"I thought you were going to call me when you arrived!"

"I thought you would check my itinerary to find out when the flight came in so you could be here on time!"

ASK has another valuable benefit—it keeps you out of the Assuming Trap, a tricky position that we've all fallen into, probably more times than we care to admit. It happens when we take actions or make decisions based on our assumptions without checking to validate them. The Assuming Trap is often in operation when there are deadline mix-ups . . . when meetings aren't cancelled that should have been . . . when meeting places are mistaken . . . whenever we think we know what others thought they should do.

You can imagine how differently the airport situation above would have turned out if one person had used STOP–HELP–ASK to confirm transportation expectations with the other.

Acting on our assumptions can be disruptive and costly—in both dollars and relationships. A CEO called for our advice regarding his district manager. He said he was surprised when this manager was upset at not receiving a bonus, when the CEO had never intended that this manager would receive a bonus. His assumption was that, due to the nature of the job description, the manager should have known he wasn't eligible for bonus participation.

The district manager, however, assumed that he was eligible because other people of his rank in the organization were receiving performance bonuses. Sadly, nobody had used STOP–HELP–ASK to discuss bonus eligibility.

The CEO felt he was being strong-armed by the district manager. The district manager felt he was being treated unfairly by being excluded from the bonus pool. Their mutually incorrect assumptions broke the trust between them, nearly causing the end of their relationship.

We were able to bring them together, using STOP–HELP–ASK to work through their disagreement. Together, we put their assumptions on the table for discussion and examined how each could have come to his expectation. As we worked with them, it became clear that neither had ever considered that he might be operating from assumptions, not reality.

The Assuming Trap can be avoided by adopting an attitude of, "I think this is so, but I need to find out." The concept of "coming alongside" someone can also make a difference: If you are on the other person's side as well as your own, neither party would let a critical aspect like a bonus be missing from such an agreement.

It took some effort for this duo to move beyond the strong feelings that their acting on assumptions had caused. Moving into the next S.H.A.R.E.™ Tools (RISK and EXPLORE, explained in future chapters) to create a resolution was tentative and slow. By continually recycling through STOP–HELP–ASK to be sure everyone had a chance to express feelings and ideas, we were able to facilitate their reaching a viable solution. Their relationship needed to be rebuilt because it really hadn't been solidified from the beginning. With STOP–HELP–ASK, they now have the Tools to do so going forward.

Internal Questions to ASK Yourself

When you ASK, be prepared to hear the answer. You may be saying, "Of course I want the answer, or I wouldn't ASK." Well, you might want an answer, but you might not want the answer you get!

In order to make the best use of STOP–HELP–ASK, we find it's a good idea to ASK yourself:

- What information do I want?

- Am I prepared to hear the answer?

- Am I prepared to make changes based on the new information I receive?

- How would I feel if someone asked me that?

- How can I prepare myself not to overreact?

And often most important:

- Does the situation warrant that I step forward or should I wait?

We are all collaborative members of our communities large and small, and with that comes a responsibility to be accountable and step forward in as collaborative and team oriented a way as possible.

If you're caught off guard or confused by an answer, or begin to feel an uncomfortable emotional response, just recycle through STOP–HELP–ASK. It can also help to remember that the goal is to understand each other and work together more effectively.

Once you've received information, here are internal questions to ASK that can HELP decide on next steps:

- Do we have enough information?

- Is everyone on the same page?

- Should I STOP and HELP make sure everything is clear for others?

- Have I made sure to ASK my partner in conversation to check if she has more questions?

- Are we ready to move forward into RISK and EXPLORE?

STOP-HELP-ASK with Friends and Family

Clients have told us that, once they learn how to use the S.H.A.R.E.™ Tools at work, they find themselves applying them in all parts of their lives. As the Tools become more and more integrated into your thoughts and speech, you'll find yourself naturally applying them.

A colleague of ours, Sasha, had been using the Tools at work for several months. After returning from vacation, she told us a story of how STOP-HELP-ASK saved a longtime friendship.

"I had been traveling for several weeks on vacation and was visiting a dear friend who had been going through some serious challenges. She met me at the airport after my long international flight. No sooner had I settled into her car than she launched into a monologue of her difficulties. 'I'm so happy you're here. I'm going crazy with this new house. We don't seem to have enough budgeted and the contractor wants a larger down payment. I want to scream because Charlie won't discuss it with me. And . . .'

"I held up my hand to indicate that this was too much and said, 'Please, please STOP. I hear you but I need your HELP to let me catch my breath from this trip. Could we talk early tomorrow morning before the others are up—as we've done for years? That way, I can focus on what you need me to hear. I am too tired tonight.' Without hesitation, my friend agreed to postpone our discussion. After a good night's sleep, we had a wonderful conversation and, with ASK, we were able to clarify the issues she had to address."

Sasha told us that she was sure that, if she had continued the conversation that night after she arrived, she might have said things she regretted, possibly damaging their friendship. What was surprising to her was that the S.H.A.R.E.™ Tools came naturally to her just when she needed them most.

Roger is the busy CEO of a large business. We had worked with him to develop better communication between his company's senior executives and the board of directors by integrating the S.H.A.R.E.™ Tools into his organization. He told us that he had started using STOP–HELP–ASK with his father, who was becoming increasingly forgetful. Roger concentrated on using an internal STOP to prevent himself from getting angry or impatient at having to repeat the same information over and over. Then, he was able to use STOP–HELP–ASK with his father:

"When I could STOP myself, I could pay better attention to Dad. My approach was to request Dad's HELP as many times as needed to engage him in our conversation. I wanted to understand what he needed. I would ASK questions until I understood what was happening. My patience reduced his stress. As his anxiety level went down, he seemed less confused and would remember longer. It's not expected that his condition will improve, but for now, he and I can enjoy this time together." Roger was surprised by how easily he was able to apply the Tools that he was using in high-level business conversations in his personal life with such powerful results.

Transitioning to RISK

ASK is a pivotal point in S.H.A.R.E.™ Tools when we decide whether or not to advance the conversation into more depth or into a creative process using RISK and EXPLORE. Sometimes, all you need to achieve your aim in a conversation is STOP–HELP–ASK. These first three Tools are useful in navigating most conversations and the many challenges that come your way. You can get information you need, make sure your conversation partners are on the same page, protect yourself and others when challenges appear, and prevent small issues from becoming problems.

Information you gather in ASK will let you know if you and others are ready to take the next step. If you need to create something new—a solution to a problem; a new service or product; a new way to work together—moving into RISK can be a good choice, as we'll discuss in the next chapter.

S.H.A.R.E.™ Tools in Action
How ASK Revealed Untapped Potential

A client of ours with many years' experience sought our support in finding a new position worthy of her many talents. It can be difficult at times to capitalize on a lifetime of experience, knowledge, contacts, and interpersonal skills, but persistence paid off in a well-deserved merger opportunity for her practice with the right new partners. Next, the challenge was agreeing on how she was going to function in her role after the merger.

During negotiations before the merger was finalized, we had diligently focused on what our client's responsibilities would be in her new business environment. It wasn't an easy question to answer, but we persisted in a patient, yet focused way. We made sure to STOP and ASK questions, to dialogue with the buyer and partners, to listen, and to EXPLORE options. We might have nagged a bit, too.

The tipping point that demonstrated our client's value came in a discussion during due diligence. A question arose about how she could participate strategically in a new opportunity. It was perfect timing to say, "We've actually been thinking about what her strategic role might be in the new structure. Is now a good time to discuss that?" We were able to remind everyone about her breadth and depth of experience, including that she held an executive position in a major national association. It became apparent to her new partners that her contacts were considerable and could contribute to the new firm's strategic imperatives for future mergers. Together, we were able to EXPLORE the new opportunity with fresh eyes and no preconceived ideas. That meeting allowed our client to position herself to contribute to long-term benefits for the firm and for herself.

Key to this collaboration was purposeful conversation. Although we used every S.H.A.R.E.™ Tool, ASK played a major role. By continuing to ASK, we gathered information and ideas that might not otherwise have surfaced. The value-added for both parties was positive and significant.

When you first start using this Tool, it can take patience to ASK enough questions to move the conversation in new directions. Most of us tend to be more interested in giving or getting specific answers than in formulating open-ended questions or creating collaborative questions that expand understanding for everyone. But inclusive questions lead to expansive answers, notions, ideas, and opportunities—which can mean more revenue and opportunity for everyone.

ASK Chapter Key Concepts

- STOP, HELP, and ASK can be tied together for maximum results.

- ASK to get clarification or more information to understand what the speaker is saying.

- ASK open-ended questions to get as much information as possible.

- ASK questions to create collaboration, not interrogation.

- Be open and willing to hear answers to questions.

• ASK may take time, but it is worth the investment.

• When formulating questions, assume a foundation of "coming alongside" others and a focus on "finding out what happened." These will help lead you to the information you did not know that you and others needed to know.

Adding Value with ASK

• ASK brings new information to light that can save time in the future, increase profits, and improve relationships.

• ASK can get everything on the table, which prevents problems and increases productivity.

• ASK engages others in adding the value of their information, knowledge, and expertise.

• ASK allows you to pose internal questions to help keep you on point and focused in conversation.

• ASK helps everyone be more on the same page.

Action Steps

• Listen for ways that people ASK questions and try to frame your own in an open-ended style.

• Notice whether you make assumptions about what someone thinks, how something will be done, or what will happen next. If you do, try to use STOP–HELP–ASK to clarify or discover whether your assumptions are correct.

• Use STOP–HELP–ASK to get a better understanding of what, how, and when as you give or receive instructions.

Your Observations

- How did others respond to your open-ended questions? Did your questions change the conversation or your relationship?

- How did the process of giving and receiving instructions change? What was different in these interactions compared to past interactions?

- How did you add value by using ASK?

- What has changed at work or in your personal life now that you've tried STOP–HELP–ASK?

Our Observations

Often, communication is focused on telling, not on understanding. "Telling" can come from a mind-set of, "I know better, so you should hear and do what I say." The S.H.A.R.E.™ Tools shift that mind-set from dueling dialogues to "partners in conversation." People become more aware of others' perspectives. Nobody knows everything. None of us knows what others are thinking or feeling or what is happening in their worlds. With STOP–HELP–ASK, we create an atmosphere for collaboration based on combined perspectives.

When our conversation partners know that we want to understand their opinions, ideas, and thoughts, they appreciate being heard and become more comfortable sharing and coming alongside others. The conversation becomes richer, more substantive, and more powerful for all.

We can demonstrate our intent to understand when we ASK questions like:

1. "I want to understand what you mean when you say . . ."

2. "Can I ask how that affects your perceptions?"

3. "Can you tell me more about what happened when . . . ?"

When the conversation started, the two of you may or may not have had different points of view. With ASK, you can add information, clarify misunderstandings, honor others' perceptions, and build a bridge to understanding. In the process, you can advance concepts and ideas, get work done, deepen relationships, and add value.

Now, you are ready to consider the possibility of moving into RISK.

CHAPTER 5

RISK—OPENING DOORS TO INFINITE POSSIBILITIES

"Only those who will risk going too far can possibly find out how far one can go."—T. S. Eliot

RISK can open doors to new ideas, possibilities, and innovations that would have never materialized without it. As you use the Tools, you'll start to know instinctively when to RISK. You'll feel a sense of momentum to present your idea, perception, or desire—or you'll feel that momentum building in others and you can increase the possibility that they will feel comfortable about taking a RISK.

Getting to RISK need not take a long time and a lot of hard work. Sometimes you can get to RISK in under a minute. Or it may not happen at all. It depends on the situation and the people you are dialoguing with to help make a RISK rewarding.

Initiating RISK can be as simple as saying, "May I take a RISK?" It's a succinct question that captures attention and can powerfully shift a conversation. If a conversation isn't reaching its potential and it doesn't seem that RISK will add value, it might be good to go back to STOP and exit the conversation. But if it seems like the time is right to consider something new, RISK will seem like just the right thing to do.

RISK is about considering change and manifesting possibilities for success. If STOP–HELP–ASK have paved the way, go for it. Some might feel edgy about this word. Have you taken risks that didn't turn out as you had hoped? Stay with us and we'll show you how RISK can be an exceptional experience.

Examples of RISK

Like the other Tools, RISK in many ways is more art than science, and it can take different forms. RISK can be posed as a question (ASK). Or it may be a declarative statement. The goal of RISK is to advance forward. Let's take a quick look at what some RISKs might look like:

> • You have a great idea about a new operational procedure but haven't had the courage to bring it up, and you don't have a clear understanding of the protocols of putting new ideas forward.

You can ask others about the protocol, but you still have to get up the nerve to raise your hand. You might say, "I've been listening to the conversation today, and an idea has been coming to me for some time. I was wondering if you might entertain the thought." Everyone acknowledges an OK. You continue: "We all know the issues with shipping and that it takes place in various parts of the factory. We've also been considering streamlining the parts department. I am wondering if we could consider consolidating the space so that parts and shipping could be in one place. Any thoughts?"

> • You are the controller for a company, and the president wants to hire a CFO.

You're pleased to be included as part of the team to select someone for this new position. As things move forward, you begin to think about ways you could add new value to the company. You realize that at some point you are going to need to take a RISK to present these new ideas to the president. You gather your nerve and ask for an appointment with the president for a short but important conversation. In the conversation you might start off with, "John, I'm a bit confused with the process for the CFO and I could use a hand. Can I ASK you a few questions?" "Sure." "Could you give me a better idea of some the duties that I have that might be transferred to the CFO? And could you help me understand who will be reporting to me?" You chat together, and finally you say that this conversation has been very helpful and that you have an idea to run by him. He says that's fine, and you say, "With the CFO coming on board, I'm wondering if I might take on some additional duties that I haven't had before. For instance, I like cost accounting, and we don't have an adequate process for that. I've also been thinking that we haven't been tracking the products and related parts that customers purchase so that we could get a better handle on inventory management and reduce our vulnerability to customers' switching to competitors' products. Do you think we can lay out a new platform for my position as we develop this new CFO position?" The president says, "Good ideas. Can we talk about them at ten on Friday?" "Great!" you say.

> • You're assisting a customer in a retail clothing store, and the customer is just not happy, despite your attentive service and support.

You now have brought him four suits, various pants and sports jackets, and six shirts without hearing a single, "I like that." Being a good trouper, you've done your STOP–HELP–ASKs and can't seem to be able to get in sync with him. Obviously it's time to shift some gears. First, you do an internal STOP and you would need to STOP the process and see if the customer will HELP by allowing you to ASK some more in-depth questions to get an expanded sense of what he is thinking and how you can assist him. So, you ASK, "I'm wondering about the last two suits and am curious if they came close to what you are looking for?" "I don't know," he says. OK, so maybe it's time for a RISK. You could say, "Can I take a bit of RISK here?" The customer agrees, and you say, "I've noticed that you seem uncomfortable with the built-up shoulders on the suits and that the pants we've tried seem to be too awkward in a subtle way. Am I on track at all?" "Well, the truth is the whole process is uncomfortable," the customer replies. "I'm in a rush and need things now, but I can't seem to make a decision." You say, "I'm thinking we might do more of a show-and-tell before we ask you to try on the clothes. I can arrange various compositions of pants, shirts, suits, ties, and even belts. Then we can talk about them, get your reactions, and select the ones you'd like to try on. Could that help?" "Great idea. Thanks!"

- **You're the president of a manufacturing company with the desire to expand through acquisition as well as internal growth.**

You have a very friendly relationship with the president of a smaller company in the same industry, a firm making specialized products. You go to the same conventions, trade shows, and conferences. You see each other socially on occasion and always have good conversations. Your intuition says that there's something here to explore. You want to engage him in a conversation, but you don't know what the unintended consequences might be—and you want to stay friends. You could ask your investment banker to make the inquiry, but that might be too impersonal. You want to take this RISK, but you want to mitigate the downside. You decide the RISK is worth it and it's time to act. At the next convention, you spot him in the exhibit hall, STOP him, and ask for his HELP with something that has been on your mind. You ask if he would be open to a confidential conversation, now or at a future meeting. "Sure, let's get some coffee and talk now," he says. Over coffee, you could say, "Can I ASK you a few questions about your new products and where you think they fit in the industry?" The talk goes back and forth and you build more of a rapport. Finally, you know you have to advance the process, so you might say, "I appreciate your sharing this information with me. It makes me more interested in chatting with you about some strategic opportunities that have been rolling around in my mind. I hope I'm not being too forthright, but I would like very much to discuss how our product lines might work together in a way that might be even more successful than the way we do it individually. Is this of any interest?" The other president replies, "I'm interested and very curious as to how you see them as complementary." The conversation can now expand its possibilities.

> • Retirement decisions and succession planning for
> businesses are issues that become important in our work
> and family lives.

Some friends of ours needed to have a serious conversation with their mother about her transitioning from work to retirement. She has been with a company for a long time and enjoyed the intellectual challenge of working. Unfortunately, her physical health was making it more difficult for her to work every day. Fortunately, our friends had developed good S.H.A.R.E.™ skills. Using STOP–HELP–ASK, they discovered their mother's interests and needs and what her plans might be. They were then able to RISK opening the topic of her transitioning from full-time employment over a period of several years.

Our friends recalled their conversation. "As we talked with Mom about what she wanted to do, she told us that she had joined a tai chi class and wanted more time for that. She was also involved in the local book club. With the grandchildren growing up, work kept her from traveling to see them as often as she'd like. As the conversation continued, she talked about other interests outside work.

"The time seemed right, so we decided to RISK opening the discussion about reducing her workload. I said, 'Mom, it sounds as if you have so much you would enjoy doing besides work. Do you think we might spend some time to understand what you would like to do in the future? In fact, I'd like to take a RISK. Would you be open to considering ways to change your work schedule so you could have more time for yourself and your interests? Could you EXPLORE that with us and how we could help?'

"I was happily surprised when she agreed to discuss working fewer hours. She told me that the idea of working less had great appeal, once she began thinking about everything she enjoyed. She appreciated how we talked it through with her instead of telling her what to do." Together, the family was able to EXPLORE possibilities and develop some plans to ensure that everyone would be ready, both emotionally and financially, to make the transition.

Though this is an example of a personal situation, the same dialogue has to take place in every company everywhere, many times a year. Whether it's between the owners or with other team members, conversations about growth, transition, and succession are always in the mix.

Reasons to RISK

STOP–HELP–ASK can take us far, but sometimes without a RISK, it's impossible to move to the next level. Let's consider when taking a RISK might be worth it:

- **CHANGING THE STATUS QUO.** You might RISK because

you have a new idea that could contribute to more success for your employer. It might be counterintuitive to the situation or threaten an accepted tradition. At the same time, it could have tremendous potential.

• RELATIONSHIP REPAIR. You have a long-term unsatisfactory relationship with an associate, a partner, a leader, a client, or a subordinate. It could be painful, uncomfortable, or abusive, and the time has come to make some changes. Taking a RISK can move a relationship to a different level where you can decide whether that relationship can be more productive and satisfactory for everyone.

• IMPROVED TEAMWORK. You have a serious misunderstanding with your management team. Misconceptions are floating around about the success of the latest special project. This might be an appropriate time to RISK, letting the team know that you are concerned about these rumors and that you have ideas about how they can work with you to create a more positive and energizing environment.

There are many moments every day to decide to take an appropriate RISK. A friend told me about a time she was working with a team of colleagues to finalize a big campaign for presentation to senior management: "We'd been meeting for weeks, and now we were in the final phases. But the account executive and the marketing director hit an impasse about some key final points. It got very intense very fast. The marketing director, a take-charge type, was extremely direct about his concerns. The account executive, a quieter, more deliberate type, was digging in his heels against the marketing director. The accounting guy was looking from one to the other in dismay.

"I figured I had nothing to lose, because if anyone walked out at that moment, this project was over. We'd been learning about the Tools, so I did a group STOP. I took a RISK and asked whether we could all get back on the same page using the S.H.A.R.E.™ Tools. Everyone agreed. We started again, but this time being careful to use the Tools as we went along. They kept us dialoguing instead of monologuing. Gradually, the discussion began to get better results. We went back and forth discussing everyone's concerns. Then the marketing director took a RISK by saying, "I think I understand what you mean. Would you consider . . ." and went on to make a suggestion.

"The change in the room was electric. The account executive understood that the marketing director just really wanted to get things right. It reframed everything. Confrontation turned into collaboration as everyone began to EXPLORE real options and arrived at a solution that reflected everyone's participation. Most important, the process rebonded the whole team."

Potential Benefits of RISK

RISK is about reward—but reward for all, not just one. Those benefits can include advancing our ideas for the betterment of a situation and/or the organization; creating a more effective relationship with our associates, management, or clients; or doing something for others and their endeavors. Some benefits are crystal clear; others reveal themselves over time. RISK helps turn routine interactions into Revolutionary Conversations™ by uncovering potential and adding momentum by being inclusive.

Ultimately, RISK can lead to what we believe is the greatest benefit in business: having our achievements valued by our customers and our colleagues. Feeling that rapport, we can relax enough to truly do our best—a precious gift for everyone.

But suppose we have a customer for whom we believe we provide exceptional service, but who continues to give us negative feedback? It may be an opportunity to RISK and, possibly, create an opening for an exceptional interaction and a great step forward.

A small business we know has a longtime customer who provides substantial revenue to the company. However, the profit margin from this customer has been eroding, and at this point the reduction is significant. In fact, it's gotten to the point where losing the customer could be a blessing. But Joe, the company president, decides that if they can retain the customer and the relationship becomes more profitable for both, it will be beneficial. Even if they learn more about the issues but the profit margin still stays the same, he theorizes, they might be able to create a more mutually satisfying way to handle the relationship. So he decides to RISK finding out what's going on with the customer.

First, Joe STOPs to realize that he needs HELP before he can ASK what's going on. He calls Craig, the customer's general manager, and sets up an appointment to discuss how the firms are working together.

At the meeting, Joe STOPs the conversation to HELP clarify how well some of his company's products are supporting Craig's manufacturing process, as a precursor to finding out whether any of the new products would be at all appropriate: "Craig, I want to STOP a minute. Could you HELP us better understand how some of our existing products fit into your current operations?" Craig replies, "Glad to, but where is this going? We've been your customer for years. You must know as much about our operation as we do."

Surprised, Joe STOPs himself a moment to consider the possibility that the customer may feel much closer to his company than he'd thought.

He then ASKs, "Craig, we hope to clarify our understanding

and make sure we're on the same page. We realized it's been a while since we inventoried the products that you manufacture and that we support for you. Can we take some time to better understand?" Craig replies, "I appreciate that, and I'd be pleased to answer any questions." "For instance," Joe continues, "Which of your product lines are we most involved with?" "That's a good question," Craig answers, "there are several. Which do you want to discuss first?"

They talk about the product lines and the support Joe's company provides. "Does this answer your questions?" Craig ASKs.

It's been a good conversation so far, and Joe sees the opportunity to RISK. He replies, "It does, thank you. I wanted to ASK, because even though we've been working together successfully for more than ten years, things are changing for all of us. We're developing new products that might help your operations, and you're developing new products we might help support. We've been wondering whether we've really been servicing your company correctly. We haven't been sure whether we're in the loop with you and your manufacturing needs. Is this is something we could talk about as well?" "Of course," Craig says. "You're a valued resource to our company. We appreciate your reaching out about how you can add value to what we're doing."

The RISK is out there, and Craig seems to be in a collaborative mood. Now Joe is on track to find out what's happening with the company, the products, and the relationship and to determine what's needed to make the business association work better for everyone.

When he moves with Craig into EXPLORE, Joe will learn that Craig's purchasing agent had been given misinformation about how to work with Joe's company and wasn't treating the company like the valued provider they are. Now Joe knows what's going on, Craig has acknowledged that they are a valued provider, and Joe is able to reinforce how valued a customer Craig's company is. Whether Craig's

company ultimately remains a customer or not, by taking a calcu-
lated RISK, Joe has uncovered new information that gives him the
opportunity to positively advance a situation. That's progress and a
good use of RISK.

This process might have unfolded more straightforwardly if Joe
and Craig were closer colleagues. Joe could have just called Craig and
said, "Craig, I'm a bit confused and I could use a little HELP. Can we
talk about how well we're supporting your company?" Craig might say
"Sure, where do you want to start" Joe might say, "This is a bit of a
RISK, but it seems that all of the protocols we put in place over the last
three years have been discontinued. We designed them together so that
we both benefited, so I'm surprised. I'm wondering if we might explore
whether we're all on the same page. What do you think?" Craig might
say, "Thanks for bringing this up. We hired a new purchasing agent and
we've been having a hard time getting him to support our vendors with
our prescribed policies. It's been a challenge, but since we hadn't heard
from you, we thought things were okay. What can we do?"

Whether the Tools are used formally or casually, they can help pull
you out of a negative pattern of action-reaction so you can EXPLORE
a better strategy. Joe set up a collaborative interaction that allowed
him and his customer to come alongside each other and replatform
their working relationship. They avoided blame, found out what was
happening, and built a much better relationship. Result: an A customer who had devolved to a C level was on the path to return to A
status—a win for all.

RISK Is a Matter of Perspective

Defining what constitutes a RISK is a matter of perception. What one
person considers risky may be insignificant to someone else. How

you perceive taking a risk and using the RISK Tool is personal to you. Your life experiences may cause you to feel uncertain in some situations. Your position in the hierarchy of the workplace can lead you to be cautious. Your level of emotional investment in a given situation can make a difference. Your organization's culture can influence whether you RISK or not. Again, what you have to say may not be perceived as a RISK to someone else. Here are some ideas or actions that some may consider risky in the business arena. What do you think?

- Making cold calls

- Discussing how a project might have done better

- Opening the dialogue in a merger

- Requesting a raise

- Seeking more support on a project

- Suggesting that someone change how they approach a task at work

- Asking for an extension on a deadline

- Giving a customer "bad" news

- Phoning a client about an overdue bill

- Seeking to find out more about how a client feels about your work

For some of us, all of these might seem perilous; for others, they might seem easy. An internal STOP can allow you a moment to consider why something feels too risky before taking the next step. Using STOP–HELP–ASK internally can sometimes clear away concerns and hesitancy in taking a RISK to move forward.

However, if you feel that you have done as much as you can to prepare yourself and others for your RISK and you are still uncomfortable, here are some considerations:

- STOP and suggest that you need some time to think about what you have heard.

- ASK a few more questions and move forward with a less challenging RISK.

- Let your partners in conversation know that you'd like to advance new ideas and ASK whether they'd be open to discussion.

- Tell your partners in conversation that you would like to take a RISK and ASK if this would be the time to do so.

- ASK more questions and, if you are still hesitant, then let them know you have more questions or ASK if they have questions. If so, you might want to list them and add them to the agenda for the next meeting.

- Simply STOP yourself. You don't have to say anything. You can regroup and get back to them later.

As we use the S.H.A.R.E.™ Tools, especially with our friends and associates, we all get more comfortable with using them. This is especially true with RISK. The results of RISK can be especially rewarding when we use it to step forward with productive, interesting ideas. With these experiences and practice, it becomes easier and easier to RISK.

A good example is a COO of a professional services firm who readily lets her team and the partners know when she needs to step forward with a new idea or suggestion. She has built a strong rapport with everyone and they trust her. When she says: "I need to take a

RISK here," everyone pays attention. She doesn't abuse the privilege and uses the rest of the Tools in normal conversation.

Seeing Opportunity for RISK

No matter how good you may become at using the Tools, they are never something to be too cavalier about. They're most powerful in generating Revolutionary Conversations™ when we assess situations carefully with an eye toward how the Tools can help. One great activity to practice is becoming aware of when a RISK is on the horizon. In the example above with Joe and Craig, it started to become clear that a RISK conversation was in the making as customer service activity for this client went up and gross margins were sliding down. Some other signals you might catch that indicate the need for a RISK could be:

- the quickly ended, brisk, or terse conversation

- the vague answer

- unusual excitement about something that might seem to you to be ordinary, or

- something totally new being presented as if out of nowhere.

In these examples there is a sense that something has been missed, that something of import is going on. A RISK may be required to take the conversation to the next level. By paying attention to the signals and using STOP–HELP–ASK, we can create a foundation of attentive conversation that makes RISK more accessible.

It can also be useful to remember that RISK isn't an "all or nothing" proposition, but more like a window of opportunity that prepares everyone to consider something new or different. With this mind-set and with the support of the other S.H.A.R.E.™ Tools, RISK will feel much more accessible and safer.

Practicing Risk

Here are a few situations where we might practice taking a RISK and move a conversation to the next level of EXPLORE.

> • When participants are in general agreement on basic information but don't seem to be moving forward, it takes a RISK with a collaborative question to determine why you aren't getting any traction. For example: "I'm wondering if we shouldn't be asking ourselves why we are not moving forward to some kind of better result."

Alex and Justin have been working on developing an employment contract. Alex, the business owner, wants Justin, the prospective new vice president of marketing, to work on a minimal base salary and a large commission. Justin is excited about the product and the company, but he knows the market is tight and that it will take him a minimum of a year to earn enough commissions to begin to meet his financial needs. To be successful, he wants a higher base salary for at least a year. After a long discussion, Justin realizes that they are not moving forward.

In order to advance the discussion, Justin knows he must take a RISK. He starts by saying, "I'm concerned about how I can accomplish my financial requirements in this market. I have been trying to figure out a way but can't seem to get there. I wonder if you could HELP me understand your perspective more specifically. Is that okay?" [ASK]. Alex agrees. They chat; then Justin takes his RISK: "Are there other ways to derive compensation in the current environment? Would you be willing to look at compensation from a different point of view?" [RISK].

Justin has extended himself by suggesting that there might be a new way to determine compensation. So that Justin can move the conversation into EXPLORE, in a perfect world Alex might say, "Sure, what do you have in mind?" Then, they can craft an arrangement that neither would have devised alone. If Alex isn't ready to consider other ideas, Justin can still circle back to STOP–HELP–ASK and continue the conversation now or at another time. He may also decide that it is time to move on to another employment opportunity.

> • As you use STOP–HELP–ASK, you get the feeling that you're in a continuous brainstorming loop and it's time to move forward into RISK.

Tasked with increasing efficiency, the marketing department has had several meetings to brainstorm process improvements and has generated a list of possibilities. Nick has been thinking that the discussion is really going nowhere. Though they have lots of ideas, the group doesn't seem to understand the urgency of the situation. Nick has been trying to get more information on the table with more and more open-ended questions. At this point he senses that the group is in a position to make some useful choices, but the conversation seems stuck in brainstorming mode. He feels the group is searching for some direction—even the department manager, Jeff, seems somewhat confused.

Nick takes it upon himself to RISK advancing the process so that they can make some decisions. He says, "Jeff, as we're talking here, I am feeling a sense of urgency and wondering if others do as well. I'd like us to consider stopping the brainstorming process [a RISK] and suggest that we might begin to summarize and consolidate all of the great ideas we've been generating. What do you think?" Relieved, Jeff says, "Thanks, Nick. I was wondering if we had enough information. We were generating such great ideas that I didn't want to interrupt the flow. It was working well, but I think you're right. We need to do something with what we've created. Good job!" Then, they begin to EXPLORE how some of the ideas overlapped and how some were synergistic. From there, they formulated action points that they could implement immediately.

- **There is a difficult situation that must move toward EXPLORE to find resolution.**

Nancy and Allen, her manager, have been at an impasse about a job offer she received from another division of the company that will require her relocating to Cincinnati. Knowing the promotion is important for Nancy, Allen wants to support her success. If she accepts the new position, he will need her to transition her role to another associate.

Nancy has not made her decision, and she and Allen have been talking around the situation for a week. It's Monday afternoon and the deadline for Nancy to accept or reject the position is a week away. Allen knows that they need to step up the discussion in order to make good decisions and be prepared to do what is right for everyone.

He says, "Nancy, do you have a few minutes? With your offer for promotion, I can imagine this is a busy time for you. But I need some HELP. Could we talk about some of the options available for transitioning your responsibilities, if and when you take the Cincinnati offer?" She agrees, and Allen continues: "Have you had time to think about the delegation of duties that needs to be addressed, or have you thought of any promotions that are in order?" "I have," Nancy replies, "But I've been so busy with other things." Allen then moves the conversation into RISK by saying, "Thanks, because I've been thinking that, even if you don't take the promotion and stay in your current position, there could be some changes we could make that will enhance the way the job duties are performed for your role. Would you be willing to invest time tomorrow or Wednesday to EXPLORE this and other options together?"

Allen opened the door to RISK by acknowledging that they needed to discuss the transition and also took a RISK to advance some new ways for the position to evolve, whether Nancy stays or not. This approach opened the door to EXPLORE forward movement, but did not put additional pressure on Nancy to make a decision.

ASK Permission—Smoothing the Transition to RISK

In the examples above, you probably noticed that there was an element of requesting permission. It can be helpful to ASK permission before opening the door to RISK. You want to be sure everyone else is ready, too. Sometimes you can tell that everyone's ready and the conversation moves forward without your having to lay a path for it. Other times, you can double-check to see if others are ready to join you as you shift into RISK. It gives everyone a chance to prepare to go forward or to acknowledge that this is not the time to make that move. In that case, you can regroup for another time or move to another topic.

Here are ways to ASK for permission to advance into RISK:

- "May I tell you something I'm thinking?"

- "I've got a lot of ideas. Is this a good time to talk about them?"

- "Given what I've heard, can we look at it in another way? I have an idea we might discuss."

- "What I need to say may seem different, but do you think we can try it out?"

- "May I take a RISK here?"

To ASK permission to RISK is like requesting HELP—it changes the tone of the conversation. This can be particularly beneficial when the subject is highly emotional on either side.

The S.H.A.R.E.™ Tools are about collaborating, not about convincing others. Permission can be an important ingredient for encouraging participation.

RISK Management

We've all been in conversations where we took a chance and said something—and the response wasn't what we expected or hoped. If we've had too many of those experiences, we can become risk averse and begin to shy away from actively participating in conversations where RISK might advance the process.

It's natural to feel concerned that what we say might cause others to be angry, not like us, dismiss us, or think us fools. However, when we don't RISK, we miss opportunities to contribute and make positive change. The S.H.A.R.E.™ Tools help mitigate potential downsides of bringing up new ideas or possibly touchy subjects. Using STOP–HELP–ASK to create a bridge or safety net can provide courage, a road map, and a sense of appropriateness to taking a RISK.

When we take our first conscious RISK, we can begin to grow and make positive changes in our lives and the lives of others. Remember

Mary who had the aggressive boss? Though she was afraid to request that he STOP, she took that first step and changed everything.

Still need encouragement to consider the idea of RISK? Consider this quote:

> "Each underestimates her own power and overestimates the other's."
>
> ~ Deborah Tannen

S.H.A.R.E.™ Tools to the Rescue!

If you've moved too far or too fast with RISK, the S.H.A.R.E.™ Tools are there for you. For instance, suppose you've advanced an idea about cutting costs in the IT department. Then you realize you didn't get all the data from accounting that you had requested. First, you STOP yourself. Then, you can say something like, "I'm thinking that the cost-cutting conversation might be premature and I would like to slow down a bit. I need some HELP. I'm still waiting for the analysis from accounting on the overhead allocations. Could I ASK you some questions now about the data I do have, or would you like to meet tomorrow?"

By going back to STOP–HELP–ASK, you have owned your situation and have begun to move to a safer position. You've let people know what has happened and also given them options for when, how, and where you can advance the conversation with more information. This is important because, again, we don't all look at a RISK in the same way.

By paying attention to how our ideas and comments might be perceived, we can sometimes protect ourselves from creating unnecessary stress and confusion. Here are some common situations that could trigger unproductive behavior or reactions.

- **Your comments in RISK could be perceived as being critical of others. This can be as simple as commenting**

**on someone's choice of business attire or as serious
as questioning their ethics. Think ahead as to what the
impact of your comments might be.**

Perhaps you notice that the marketing department is really on top
of preparing the campaign for this year's holiday promotion. Unfortunately, that hasn't always been the case. Gregg, the department
head, is a close business associate with whom you normally might
feel comfortable just saying what's on your mind. It would be so easy
to say, "Gregg, the holiday promo campaign looks amazing! You guys
are so on top of it this year!" But you remember how stressed Gregg
was last year because pulling together the holiday campaign was so
chaotic. That's a signal warning you to advance considerately, maybe
cautiously. Instead of making a statement that carries some RISK,
you could circle back and use the S.H.A.R.E.™ Tools. You would
STOP yourself by acknowledging to yourself the possible sensitive
nature of this circumstance. Then, you could advance with something like, "Gregg, HELP me out. This promo campaign is terrific,
and your team is so together. As one manager to another, I'm curious
what you're doing to get such great results." After he tells you about it,
then you might take a RISK by saying, "I may be wrong, but it seems
to me your team is way ahead of where they were with the campaign
last year. Was that something you addressed with them specifically
this year?"

Gregg sees that you're genuinely interested in his work and skills
as a manager, and you continue with a good conversation.

This simple example demonstrates the value of the Tools even in
everyday conversations of all kinds.

- **With RISK, your comments might back a person into a
corner with perceived accusations or demands.**

An issue between Susan and Warren is that he often misses deadlines. They both work long hours and have agreed that, minimally, he will focus on meeting his responsibilities for sales reporting. Though Warren tries, he misses the deadlines more often than not, even when Susan reminds him. Well, it has happened again and Susan would just love to say, "Warren, you forgot to submit the sales reports again! Are you ever going to get this right? If this keeps up, we both might end up out of jobs!" That would back Warren into a corner and would more than likely make him feel angry and guilty, which would be a lose/lose situation.

Susan's first signal is, of course, her anger. When she STOPs herself from blurting out her feelings, she realizes that she has never understood why this happens: how can Warren be so consistently late with the reports?

Susan realizes she needs some HELP. She then goes into an internal ASK mode: "What don't I know? Where does sales reporting fit into Warren's priorities? Is there something I can do to support him? It's time to talk."

She calls Warren to request a meeting about a number of topics she'd like to discuss. When they meet, she begins discussing her agenda topics. When they reach the issue of sales reporting, she says, "Warren, our discussion is going well but I need to STOP. I need HELP understanding some things regarding the sales reporting. I know this is touchy, but we missed the deadline again. I need some HELP now. Could you HELP me better understand how we are continually missing our deadlines?"

"We do need to talk about this," Warren replies. "It disturbs me, too. Frankly, I don't have time to produce the reports. I worked sixty-five hours last week and am on track to do the same this week, and much of my time this week was spent on your special projects. We have the new cash management/accounts payable system, the new payroll processing software that goes live on January first, and the new travel expense reporting that is now weekly. These are killing me. The projects we're doing together, along with my normal duties, make it almost impossible to do everything. On top of that, it would be great if I could set up a more automated system so I wouldn't have to spend so much time creating the reports. I'm not complaining—I love my job. This issue has been on my mind, but I haven't had time to think or tell you what I've been going through. I also see all the new projects you've been given and I don't want to bother you. I'm sorry. I should have come to you."

With all this out on the table, Susan can now use STOP–HELP–ASK to begin to solve the problem together. She says, "Warren, I hear you. I want you to know that I believe we can resolve this situation together. We do need to make sales reports a priority. I would like to suggest that we get together—but I want to take the time to do this right. It might HELP you with your heavy workload. Would you be okay with that?" "I'd appreciate that," he says. Susan continues, "Okay, can we invest time tomorrow to begin to get a better handle on making this work better for everyone? Can we meet in the conference room at seven a.m. with a list of your key duties and what support you need?" "Will do," Warren says, "thanks for taking the time."

Now, these two are on the path to EXPLORE ways to resolve their work challenges. With the S.H.A.R.E.™ Tools, they were able to RISK telling it like it is in an honest, constructive manner and begin to agree about a way to meet their deadlines.

> • With RISK, an idea could substantially change the status quo. Your idea may be the perfect solution from your perspective, but it could threaten someone else's position or way of working.

Heidi, a new marketing director, is frustrated that invoices from her vendors are always paid late. At her previous company, this was never a problem because there was a fast-track payment system for invoices up to a certain amount for approved vendors. But Brad, the controller at her new employer, has always looked at every invoice and personally approved all of them. When the business was smaller, that method worked, but it had grown dramatically over the last three years.

Heidi would like to tell Brad that they should adopt the system from her previous company so that her department could run more smoothly, but she also realizes that she has to use STOP internally to slow down and get a better handle on the dynamics of the situation. She is new to the company. Brad is the controller and an owner, too. Just because this system worked in the other company doesn't mean it will work here. She decides that she must approach Brad with the intent of having a constructive discussion.

She sets an appointment to meet with Brad to discuss accounts payable. At their meeting, she remembers the S.H.A.R.E.® Workshop from her former employer. "Brad, could I have some time with you? I need some HELP to get a better understanding of how the bill paying process works." Brad agrees to spend some time with her and she uses STOP–HELP–ASK to get a clear understanding of the current billing process. Heidi takes a RISK by saying, "Brad, this has been very helpful, but I'm wondering if we could talk about a process that has worked very well for me in other companies. Would that be okay?"

Now she and Brad can begin a dialogue about how a priority vendor system might be beneficial to everyone. By creating a STOP–HELP–ASK conversation with Brad, Heidi doesn't imply that he isn't doing his job well, and she lays the foundation for being able to RISK suggesting ideas. Brad still may not accept them, but the point is that he's listening, and there's no animosity or negative fallout from the process.

RISK Recovery

Sometimes, despite our best intentions, we blunder headlong into RISK. Maybe everything's going along fine—and then we blow it. Good news—we're all human and it happens to all of us. Better news—the Tools can support your recovery.

Matthew and Samantha are coworkers at a small start-up. They've been working for months to get a meeting with a major prospect, and finally they've succeeded. As it turns out, the prospect is coming to town for a few days. The only time he has available is for a Saturday lunch. They set the date.

The office where Matthew and Samantha work is a fast-paced, casual place where everyone wears jeans and T-shirts. Samantha's been the main contact with this prospect, and she knows he's a buttoned-down type—but as Friday rolls around and she and Matthew get ready to head home after work, she realizes she may not have communicated this to Matthew. As they're leaving the office, she says to him, "You are dressing up tomorrow, right?" Matthew hears, "You aren't going to look as grubby as usual, are you?" Samantha gets a withering look and realizes that she's landed in RISK without seeing it coming.

With the S.H.A.R.E.™ Tools, she can recover with STOP–HELP–ASK, saying something like, "I'm sorry, that didn't come out right. Could we start over?" With a chance to try again, she might say, "I need to be clear about what I'm thinking. With everything that's been going on, I don't think I told you that I get the feeling from talking to this guy that his business style is pretty traditional. So I'm wondering if we need to dress up a bit even though it's a weekend appointment.

What do you think?" Matthew might say, "I want to be sure that the client is comfortable, too, but I don't want to wear a business suit and present ourselves or the company in a totally artificial way. What do you think if we call the client tomorrow and suggest Casey's Pub?"

Samantha could follow up with, "That could work, but for our first meeting I'd prefer a restaurant that's quieter and not quite that casual. Could we plan the pub for a future meeting? How about the new Seafood Grill? It's getting some buzz around town, and we'll be fine in business casual clothes." Matthew agrees: "Okay, that sounds good."

Samantha was able to recover from her unwitting plunge into RISK with a simple STOP and an acknowledgment that she hadn't communicated her intentions well. It gave her a chance to go back and work toward a clearer understanding.

If you realize you've jumped into RISK and you're out there on your own, first use an internal STOP to take a quick inventory of what you've seen, heard, or sensed. Who knows, you might be the only one who thinks you reached too far! Then, shift back down to STOP–HELP–ASK to find out more. There are gracious ways to regroup and repair. Here are a few suggestions:

> • "Let me STOP for a moment. Is this new information for you? Could we talk about it so I can understand what you are thinking?"

> • "I feel that I didn't present my idea clearly. I could use some HELP to understand more about what your view might be. How do you feel about that?"

> • "Sorry, it looks as if I've jumped ahead and may have missed some important details. Could we go back to discuss more about the situation? What were some of the areas I might clarify?"

Eventually, using the Tools, you may find another way to enter RISK.

RISK on the Job

Katie, the office manager of a midsize law firm, knows that the firm has an important case coming up. At the same time, she knows that the partners are committed to implementing a document management system to establish a paperless environment. In order to accomplish both tasks and ensure that nothing falls through the cracks during the case, she believes that they will need to hire a file clerk during the paperless transition. In the past, Andy, a managing partner, has said that he is not interested in hiring new administrative staff. Katie, being the savvy office manager she is, has been a student of the Tools. She knows that it's important to take some time to discuss the case, the paperless project, and the possible need for an additional file clerk.

Katie approaches Andy, making sure he has time to talk with her. She begins the conversation with an update on the current document management conversion, keeping it simple and concise. Andy comments that everything needs to be complete before the case starts in two months. Katie is concerned that the deadline will not be met without extra staff. First, to be sure she understands the implications and the demands of this case, she uses STOP, HELP, and ASK. She and Andy exchange information with a focus on the importance of success in the upcoming case. Because of the foundation created by STOP–HELP–ASK, Katie feels ready to introduce the idea of additional staff.

Katie says, "This case is an opportunity for the firm, and I understand how important it will be to capture all documents electronically. I'm wondering if you would be interested in reviewing resource requirements to see if we have enough people. Could we do that [ASK]?" Andy says, "Do you want to start with associates or administration?" She answers, "How about administration, and please let me tell you why. I have been thinking that we might need one or more file clerks. I want to make sure we don't miss anything. I want to do a resource analysis to be sure our assumptions about staffing are correct [RISK]."

Andy responds, "I don't know. Adding staff would mean more nonbillable people, and we've been watching the budget closely. I thought the associates could do it."

Katie taps into the Tools and says, "I understand and concur with your goal of using the associates [STOP]. I need your HELP to understand how much time you anticipate it will take to scan those documents. I estimate that it could be as much as three to four hours a day for the associates to do the filing, maybe more. How does that fit into your estimates [ASK]?"

Andy responds, "I didn't think it would take more than an hour. That's a lot of billable time that we would lose at their rate. Assuming it takes three to four hours per day for the associates to do it, how long would it take with a clerk?"

Katie continues, "That's what I'd like to find out. With our estimates so far apart, do you think we could reconsider my idea of doing a resource analysis? We might be able to do a sample to get a better idea of what is needed. Could we EXPLORE more details?"

And they are off and running.

RISK to Save Yourself

When the situation is emotional, in order to move beyond whatever is causing distress, we can use STOP–HELP–ASK to shift the conversation into RISK and then EXPLORE. Without RISK to help us find new ways to understand situations or create new options, we will likely continue in the same unproductive cycle.

Amanda, a staff member in a client's business, was having difficulty with her supervisor. In fact, her job was in jeopardy, and we were coaching her. Amanda was sent out with a supervisor we'll call Ron to gather data at a client office. This was a new experience for Amanda, and she was nervous. On the way over, Ron rushed through the instructions, talking quickly. At the client's office, Amanda did her best but got confused. She feared going back to Ron with questions because she expected him to think she was incapable of doing the job. She spent the morning struggling to figure things out.

When she and Ron met at midday, she tried to ask her questions, but he didn't listen carefully to what she said. He gave her some additional quick instructions and informed her that the client would be angry if the job took too long, so she needed to get back to work.

At this point, Amanda was near tears. She was afraid to disappoint her supervisor and worried that she would cause client problems. She was so upset that she couldn't think what to do.

This whole story came up the next day when Amanda was still upset and her coworkers requested that a manager check in with her. Many aspects of this situation needed attention, but Amanda was our focus. In order to grow professionally and personally, she needed to find a way to be heard and to use this situation as an opportunity to learn how to handle this kind of challenge better in the future.

As a starting point, she needed to use STOP: first, to STOP her emotions from getting the best of her; then, to STOP Ron so she could get his cooperation and the information she needed. We coached her in using these first steps and saw her confidence improve. This was important because she and Ron would be working together in the future.

We knew that Ron was a tough character who believed, "People in this business need to have a thick skin." If Amanda was going to establish a way to work with him, she would have to RISK. We role-played the situation with her to prepare her for the discussion. Here's one way it could go:

Amanda starts with, "Ron, do you have a minute to talk about the job last week?"

Ron says, "I've only got a few minutes, but come on in. You were terrible on that job."

Amanda does an internal STOP to calm her fear and advances the conversation with, "I know it didn't go well. That's why I wanted to talk with you—so we don't repeat this. I need your HELP to figure out how we can work better together."

Ron says, "I told you how to do it."

Amanda remains calm and responds, "Yes, you did give me that list. I thought I understood it but it became less clear as I started. I want to do a good job. And, like you, I want to make sure our clients are satisfied."

Ron says, "Well, that's one thing we can certainly agree on."

Amanda has been able to establish a small but meaningful foundation. She decides to take a RISK: "I'm wondering if you might be open to discussing other ways we could prepare for working with clients."

Ron, willing to give a little, says, "We need to figure something out. If you'd listen to what I tell you, we'd be fine."

Amanda takes a further RISK: "You know, I was listening carefully. But I later realized that I didn't completely understand. I'm new in this position. I need your knowledge and experience sometimes to help me connect the dots. If we can find a way to do this so it doesn't disrupt your schedule, would you be open to taking more time with me to answer questions while I'm learning?"

If Ron agrees to this, Amanda might say, "Thanks, Ron. I appreciate your willingness to work with me. I know you only had a few minutes to talk today. Could we set up a short meeting later in the week to figure out the best way for me to ASK questions?"

At this point, Amanda has shown that she's a professional who understands what's expected of her and can take charge of her own learning needs. She has gained strength and confidence in herself and her ability to manage difficult situations, and she's created a foundation to improve Ron's confidence in her. Amanda had to RISK to save her self-respect and her career. This was not a time to Exit Stage Left and leave it at that. To resolve this situation, RISK was a necessity.

RISK Reverse

Although Amanda's situation was on its way to resolution after she took a RISK, sometimes it's appropriate to consider not choosing RISK and instead opt for a Complete STOP—Exit Stage Left. If you've tried working through the Tools and are finding that the other person is unwilling to participate, one of you is highly emotional, or the chemistry is not right, you may decide not to RISK opening a topic or presenting a new idea. Instead, you might do a gracious STOP with the conversation and resume it at another time.

Added Value with RISK

RISK can be very valuable, but it requires paying close attention to the conversation and situation. It can entail patience to stay the course with STOP–HELP–ASK until there is enough information on the table, but it's worth it in many cases, since RISK is where we can have significant impact and add tremendous value.

Some of the value we add in RISK comes from ourselves. If we've been using STOP–HELP–ASK, we've been gathering additional data to augment what we already think we know. This new information can magnify our ideas and generate new ideas from others. This alone can change how business is done and how individual relationships work.

We also add value by demonstrating courage and thoughtfulness when we step forward and respectfully seek to change the status quo. In doing so, we make it safe for others to RISK, to express their thoughts and share new ideas. Everyone's enthusiasm builds.

In the example earlier in this chapter about the account executive and the marketing director working on an important campaign, the tangible value was resolution of a thorny, high-stakes problem. The deeper value was the strength that developed in the team because someone was able to RISK. That RISK created a way to foster trust and community among the team that would transcend the project.

In the example of Amanda and Ron, Amanda's willingness to RISK was valuable to her on a personal level, but she also made a significant contribution to the firm. Because of her RISK, Ron began considering a different way to work with people, which could reduce employee turnover, short and long term. Their work with clients began to run more smoothly and profitably, too. Amanda's RISK wasn't easy, but it benefited everyone.

S.H.A.R.E.™ Tools in Action

How RISK Paid Off for Everyone

A three-owner engineering firm contacted us because it was having growing pains. They had two offices—one smaller and one larger—and a client that represented more than 25% of their revenue. The partners were not seeing eye to eye about how to grow the firm. What had started as a period of terrific advancement had degenerated into debate and stalemate.

We knew immediately we had to address communication within the firm. We held a one-and-a-half-day training program on the basic S.H.A.R.E.™ Tools.

A week later, we had every employee complete a confidential written survey. We then interviewed staff members individually. During the two weeks after the training session, the staff had gotten together to plan what they thought would help the firm. Unanimously, they wanted to run operations—something they had begun to articulate in our one-on-one interviews. They knew this was a RISK but felt strongly that it would improve the firm dynamics.

We proposed the concept of the staff running the operations. The partners were very enthusiastic. We crafted an incentive program for everyone in the firm that allowed everyone's participation in all aspects of client need, client work allocation, chargeability, and profits. The essential ingredient was that this program created a true team environment with good chemistry and everyone's buy-in.

While staff team members were assuming responsibility for the firm, we were able to come to grips with the challenges about growth among the owners. The S.H.A.R.E.™ Tools allowed us to see what would happen if two of the three partners left and the offices were consolidated into a single location. That decision was a significant RISK that we could not have advanced unless the employees had taken their own RISK by expressing their desire to run the firm.

This was a RISK success story. Dissenting partners removed themselves from the equation. Initially, with a single remaining office, total revenue was cut substantially. But the team members and their incentive plan advanced the growth of the firm: within eighteen months, the business was on its way to doubling, and profitability was up. With the S.H.A.R.E.™ Tools as a foundation for communication and with a team approach to growing the business, it was as if a new firm had been created. As team members came alongside each other with their own language—the S.H.A.R.E.™ Tools—and implemented their own formula for success, they bonded as never before and together created a new business landscape.

RISK Chapter Key Concepts

• RISK is where new ideas and issues can be expressed.

• STOP–HELP–ASK prepares a foundation so participants are ready to hear new ideas.

• Depending on responses to new ideas, use STOP–HELP–ASK to gain more information or move to EXPLORE.

• Be prepared to consider a different point of view regarding a new idea, even your own.

• Telling people you are taking a RISK opens possibilities for real conversation.

Adding Value with RISK

• RISK is a shifting point that opens a door to develop opportunities.

• RISK often opens up the dialogue to ideas others might have by taking that first step toward a new idea.

• RISK helps put something new on the table so that it can be expanded on in many ways.

• RISK feels good because it means you are involved and advancing the process.

Action Steps

- Listen to discussions and interactions and see what happens when someone interjects a new idea or controversial issue. Consider how the S.H.A.R.E.™ Tools could advance the process. Then, experience it. Jump in and try STOP–HELP–ASK; then RISK to experience for yourself what happens.

- Think of a conversation that you're concerned about. Consider how you could use STOP–HELP–ASK to reach a moment where you can introduce a new idea or discuss a difficult issue. Once you've thought through a potential conversation, find a way to begin the conversation and try out the Tools. Pay attention to others and to what's going on inside you. For instance, your palms may get sweaty, your mouth may get dry, or you may have butterflies in your stomach. You don't need to pick the most difficult issue on your list. Test the Tools to see how they work.

- When you have success using RISK, you'll try it again and again. After experiencing the positive results of RISK, you will be more comfortable in future conversations to try RISK again.

Your Observations

1. Observe how conversations flow and what happens when you RISK.

2. With STOP–HELP–ASK–RISK, how can you remind yourself to use the S.H.A.R.E.™ Tools more often?

3. Notice how ideas that evolve from RISK can take on a life of their own and can enhance the environment for everyone.

Our Observations

Mary Parker Follett, the pioneering management guru whom we introduced in chapter 1, set the stage for how we might think about moving into RISK. She suggested that we ask ourselves: "What are others thinking? Where does my thinking mesh with theirs? Where does it differ? How might we integrate the thinking of all to give birth to new ideas?" With these kinds of questions at the forefront, RISK becomes part of the natural progression of a conversation—a step forward to create new and more positive outcomes for everyone. RISK is a powerful, positive opportunity to seek out rather than avoid.

We always have the opportunity to choose to RISK or not; our conversation partner has the option to join or not. There's no flashing light that tells us it's time to move forward. We find that, when we trust our intuition and observations, we can decide how and when to step forward with RISK. You may have what you think is a perfect idea; then, seeing your boss's jaw tighten and his posture change, you may decide it's not the time to speak up. Or you may see those same signals as an opportunity to advance the conversation. Or, if you begin to feel your emotions rise and know that you cannot continue the conversation in a positive way, you can use your Exit Stage Left STOP and come back to the discussion later.

RISK is not required in every conversation, but it's always available to you when you need it. RISK is your choice.

CHAPTER 6

EXPLORE—TRANSFORMING POSSIBILITIES INTO REALITIES

E XPLORE is where the dialogue builds something for everyone, bringing a true return on our conversational investment. It's a stimulating experience where everyone can convert possibilities into opportunities and realities that hadn't existed before. Here are a few examples of RISK possibilities being transformed into EXPLORE opportunities:

- The RISK: A radical idea to maximize success with the merger of your company. In EXPLORE, you convene a special task group to define details and plans for next steps. This opportunity could make a substantial difference in the organization's future.

- The RISK: An HR department launches a survey to evaluate employee satisfaction with HR's services. After the results are tallied, the HR director and her team use EXPLORE to craft new initiatives to improve employee satisfaction and open doors for more engagement and productivity.

- The RISK: Pitching an innovative product/service launch to your conservative leadership. In EXPLORE, you can examine all opinions and perspectives and create a plan with buy-in from everyone. Then action points can be put in place to maximize all the good ideas.

In each of these examples, EXPLORE can help create a new view of a future that may never have been anticipated.

Stepping into EXPLORE

EXPLORE can take a few minutes or hours. It depends on how engaged participants are and how quickly a solution or a resolution is needed or can be reached. A driving force behind the effectiveness of EXPLORE is how clear and impactful the RISK is. The more honest and forthright the RISK, the more compelling and proactive EXPLORE can be. Getting to EXPLORE may take time, energy, and the courage to make a sincere and honest RISK. But it's exciting to feel how involved people can be to find resolution and satisfaction in EXPLORE. Once ideas and collaboration begin, things may never be the same—they will be better:

- You think of a new way to manage cash that reduces the need for additional funding.

- You help resolve miscommunication between people or departments that increases productivity and enhances teamwork.

- You create a new business plan that allows owners to support a new program for growth.

- You find a niche in your business experience that creates a new career path or opportunity to learn and develop new skills.

EXPLORE works with major situations and in day-to-day, moment-to-moment interactions. Even brief encounters using EXPLORE can add up to major savings in time, resources, energy, and money or increased revenue and profitability.

When we were developing this book, we found that we had to take more time to clarify what EXPLORE conversations were really like. Because EXPLORE is the most fluid of the five Tools, Mark and Noal were having difficulty explaining how EXPLORE worked. Here's how their conversation went:

Mark: "I keep feeling that the EXPLORE chapter lacks energy and focus. Can you help? Noal: "Sure. Can you give me an idea of what you mean by lack of energy?"

Mark: "When I read the STOP, HELP, and ASK chapters, they describe specific actions that I can picture myself doing. I don't get that feeling when I read EXPLORE. Are you experiencing anything similar?"

Noal: "Well, we both know that once people are engaged with RISK, the conversation accelerates and it becomes more difficult to identify and describe the dynamics. So, I'm getting a similar picture to yours. I think the reason the EXPLORE chapter has no energy is because we have poorly defined the experience. I'm taking a RISK here, but I'm wondering if we let the conversations in our examples flow the way they naturally do in the workshops and in real life, we can frame them with short analyses of how STOP–HELP–ASK work within them."

Mark [after thinking about this a minute]: "That seems right. When I use EXPLORE, it's a bit of a blur. The only thing I often remember is that it was a success. In the book, we need to be better at describing it. Are we on the same page?"

Noal: "I agree it can be a blur and we need to rethink the chapter. But our deadline for the sample manuscript we want to send to our prepublication readers is right around the corner."

Mark: "Little HELP, I'm unclear with where you're going. What might you be suggesting?"

Noal: "Reworking the chapter seems like a lot of work, and our deadline is really close. Any thoughts?"

Mark: "As we've been talking, I'm thinking we might take a two-step approach. The EXPLORE chapter isn't bad; it's just not as energized as the others. How about we spruce up the existing examples for the readers' manuscript? Then, with their feedback, we can do a full revision later. Would that work?"

Noal: "You know what? We're having an EXPLORE conversation right now! Maybe we can use the next three to four weeks to really look at how we have these conversations. Then we can integrate our new insights along with the readers' feedback. How about it?"

Mark: "Okay, let me summarize. You're going to work a little more on the EXPLORE chapter. Then I'll take a shot at drilling down on the case examples. Then we'll finalize the manuscript and get the readers' version out on time. In the meantime, I'm going to start practicing describing EXPLORE conversations in a better way—including the one we've just been having. That sound right?"

Noal: "Perfect."

As you can see, Mark and Noal go back and forth using STOP–HELP–ASK to expand on what's being said, taking a RISK along the way to advance the process. This back-and-forth but ever-advancing dynamic is what makes EXPLORE so powerful: it helps each person continually build the conversation so that things come together at a whole new level of success and satisfaction. This was a difficult situation that needed to be resolved. Mark and Noal needed to make a shift. They did that through their commitment to being on each other's side, collaborating and not getting into my idea/your idea, respecting each piece of input, and helping the input come together into a comprehensive and valuable result.

This might be a good time to reflect again on the ideas of Mary Parker Follett. As you look at Noal and Mark's conversation, you can see it was an interaction based on Power With, not Power Over. With that as their basis, they avoided conflict and supported creativity and accomplishment. And when we look at their conversation from Follett's Law of the Situation perspective, we see that it demonstrates that new ideas, solutions, resolutions, and future achievements come from within the situation, from the information available, and from the energy of the individuals involved. EXPLORE and the rest of the Tools help bring it all together.

What EXPLORE Is . . . and Isn't

EXPLORE is a building process with take-action outcomes: Mark and Noal walked away with a new plan for getting the manuscript out to readers on time, a different perspective on how to present a problematic chapter, and a to-do list for each. What more could one ask?

It's sometimes easy to view EXPLORE as brainstorming. But brainstorming is more an idea-generating process than a conversation-based process for orchestrating solutions on the spot. A friend once said, "Brainstorming is like a wind storm—ideas going in every direction like leaves in the wind." EXPLORE and the S.H.A.R.E.™ Tools can build on brainstorming but also build upon themselves by connecting ideas and people to create something like a new reality, if you will. Both processes have their place and usefulness.

Ben, a business associate, told us about a meeting he had with a longtime colleague that points up the distinction between brainstorming and EXPLORE: "Tim asked me to lunch to brainstorm about getting important information out to industry groups that we both work with. As Tim was telling me his idea, I used STOP–HELP–ASK to clarify, but mostly I was listening to him explain his idea. As we were leaving our lunch, he thanked me for a great meeting.

"Then it dawned on me that we had shared all this information and did not have a solid plan. I took a RISK and said, 'Tim, I'm uncomfortable walking away from a conversation as good as this without developing an action plan. What do you think?' He agreed and we began to EXPLORE, discussing what we'd learned from our conversation and adding new ideas about where it might lead. I discovered that he wanted a larger audience than originally discussed. I asked, 'What do you think of using a webinar? I've presented a webinar with another colleague that drew over two hundred attendees.' He said, 'I've never presented in a webinar, but it seems like an option. Let's try it. Would you take the lead?' I said I'd be glad to.

"Walking to our cars, we came up with another idea: leveraging information from the webinar into a series of articles. As we ended our conversation, I agreed to call the webinar group to set up a presentation within the next quarter.

"With EXPLORE as our focus, we changed what could have been just a pleasant brainstorming meeting into plans for a joint webinar presentation, plus a series of joint articles that would be valuable business development opportunities."

When EXPLORE Is Needed Most

EXPLORE can save the day, helping everyone build a new platform up and out from whatever is holding back a situation or an interaction.

Getting Unstuck

Noal discovered how EXPLORE could shift situations in a stalled interaction with a long-term client.

The client is a professional services firm that's rapidly changing as long-term partners are retiring and newer partners are taking on additional responsibilities. In this fast-moving environment, Lou, the new managing partner, has to learn quickly and adapt to these changes.

It's been about a month since Noal's last contact with Lou, and it's time for a follow-up call and the implementation of changes previously agreed to. On the call, Noal attempts to move the process forward by suggesting they get together and map out next steps. Her reception is less than favorable and she's unable to meet her objective of scheduling the meeting.

This is an unusual outcome, since Lou and Noal have worked together for years and are also good friends. So much has been done in the past to move things forward that this lull in the process is significant. In addition, they had agreed a month earlier to have a meeting to check in at the thirty-day point.

Noal knows something needs to be done, but she agonizes over how to bring this up with Lou and how the conversation will go. We've all been there. We know we have to show up and embrace a tough situation, but we'd just love to avoid it in any way possible.

This is clearly a time for a Revolutionary Conversation™. This break in momentum might mean anything from burnout to the need for more direction to the need for additional resources. They won't find out unless they can EXPLORE.

She calls Lou and asks: "Lou, do you have time to talk again?" "Of course," he replies. Noal continues, "I appreciate our last call, but I'm stopped, sort of dead in the water. I need some HELP. Can I ASK you a few questions?" "Okay," Lou answers. "I assume this is important?" 'Yes," Noal confirms. Then she advances the conversation:

Noal: "A month ago, I thought we'd established the next steps in developing a new firm platform so that you could hire a COO. Am I incorrect about that?"

Lou: "Noal, you are correct."

Noal: "Okay, thanks. Can you tell me what happened in the last conversation, because it felt like everything just evaporated. I thought I was following up on what we agreed to. Can you HELP?"

Interestingly, Lou, who has been to several S.H.A.R.E.® Workshops, advances the RISK here:

Lou: "Noal, this is one of those touchy-feely conversations that I'm just bad at. I'm a process kind of guy—get things done and move on."

Noal: "Yes, this is a bit of a touchy-feely conversation. Would you be interested in having one with me now so we can move on and get things done?"

Lou: "Okay, that's cute, but these conversations are so hard for me. But you're right—it does seem like we need to get unstuck. So let's talk."

Noal: "I remember you saying in our last conversation that things had changed a bit and that you weren't ready to talk about it. I also remember you mentioning that one of the partners-to-be is having some second thoughts, but you felt uncomfortable about talking with him about the situation."

Lou: "That's correct. I couldn't face him or articulate what was happening. I stopped dead! And that threw me. How am I going to be managing partner if I can't have a touchy-feely conversation with those close to me? Then on top of that, I couldn't seem to interact with you."

Noal [a bit surprised by his forthrightness, but also relieved to understand more about the problem, decides to take a RISK]: "Well, let's have a touchy-feely conversation about all this, okay?"

Lou: "I can try."

Noal [moving into EXPLORE]: "Good. Let's start with exploring what a touchy-feely conversation is and seeing how we can make those conversations work for us. If we can make them work for you and me, you can make them work for you with others. [Then she takes another RISK]: You know, one thing we might do is to initiate conversations by asking each other whether this is a touchy-feely moment and then we can decide to go there or not. Could that work?"

Together, Noal and Lou continued to EXPLORE how they could work through the issues that had come up in this conversation, and then how to get back on track with the project. Together, they brought new issues to light that had been holding back progress, reopened blocked communication lines between the two of them, and transformed what had started as a charged situation into a bonding event. They now have common ground that they didn't have before and a plan for moving forward—and touchy-feely conversations don't need to be such a stumbling block for Lou.

Getting All the Egos in the Room

Marvin is the president of a company in a serious situation: one of its divisions is in jeopardy. This division has lost several key members over a short period of time. When this happened a few months ago, Marvin committed to support Rick, the division president, in bringing order and productivity back to his operation. Marvin requested that Pam, the general manager of another division, work with Rick to bring all special projects and production runs back to normal.

Several months later, Rick and Pam are working together and things are progressing, but it seems to be slow and effortful. Rick has been complaining that Pam and her team don't make enough time available and that they seem unmotivated. Pam and her managers feel they're doing the best they can.

Marvin realizes that he needs to come alongside this situation and help these two busy senior executives further integrate their working process. Using HELP and ASK, he requests a meeting with Rick and Pam to understand and clarify the situation and see if he can be of assistance.

At their meeting, it's clear that Rick and Pam get along and that things have been accomplished. So, what's wrong? Marvin takes a RISK: "The ingredients are here to make this work. Am I correct?" They agree. "Then maybe we might address how each team has a unique way of working [RISK]. Can we EXPLORE that possibility?" With a RISK of their own, Rick and Pam acknowledge that they never looked at it that way. With this acknowledgment, they take a great step forward in the conversation and generate good grist for the mill for EXPLORE.

They EXPLORE the situation in more depth. Marvin keeps the conversation between Rick and Pam going by using STOP–HELP–ASK to pose collaborative questions for everyone to consider. It turns out that while the two get along and share the goal of saving the division, they're working together not as a team, but more as two independents trying to succeed separately in their own unique ways, not seeing the process as a joint effort. One team was more collaborative, following up with each other; the other team was more independent and self-contained. Rick and Pam were each relying on what worked for them and their team, not realizing that those methods might not be as effective for other teams, or when those teams were working together.

Using EXPLORE, they come up with action points to help both teams work collaboratively to turn around the division. They use RISK to advance ideas for designing group incentives, establishing a progress-monitoring process, and managing team meetings. Rick and Pam set up regular meetings away from the office where they can review what's happening and use STOP–HELP–ASK for clarification. They review their own job duties to compare how each handles responsibilities differently—not to determine whose approach is right or wrong, but to better join forces. Rick plans to introduce Pam to several key customers so she can better understand their needs. They also decide to involve their team members, engaging them in a dialogue about what's been happening and asking for HELP in making plans going forward.

Rick and Pam come away from this experience better managers and leaders. Most important, their divisions are poised to perform better than ever, thanks to Marvin's skill of bringing collaboration to the situation.

Seizing Opportunity for a Revolutionary Conversation™

The following example shows how EXPLORE can have big payoffs in what might begin as a casual conversation.

After one of our S.H.A.R.E.® Workshops on sales and marketing, Brenda, one of the participants, stopped on her way out to chat with Mark: "Mark, good class! We got some really positive feedback. It looks like the younger staff saw it as an eye-opening experience. The more experienced team members seemed to concur with the ideas but felt that they instinctively practice some of these techniques."

Mark heard two things in Brenda's statement: praise for the workshop on the one hand, and a criticism, however subtle and perhaps unintended, on the other. He decided to take a RISK and ASK for more information:

"Thanks!" he said. Then: "Could you HELP by expanding on what the managers mean by saying they instinctively practice some of the Tools? If I understand you, you're saying they already knew these techniques. What do you think might be missing from the workshop for them?" "They feel that they market successfully already," Brenda replied.

Mark continued with ASK: "Do you think that we didn't tie the conversational skills well enough to marketing and sales techniques? One of the most successful role-plays of the day demonstrated how, in just a minute, the client went from 'No' to 'That's a great idea. How can I help?' " "That's true," Brenda answered, moving into RISK: "But maybe it was too subtle. What do you think?" "Maybe so," Mark said, continuing into EXPLORE: "In the next class, should we discuss what marketing means to them and come up with a common under-standing? That way, maybe all of us will get a better sense of how this technology could be applied to their marketing efforts. Do you think that would work?" "Yes," Brenda replied, "I think would help." Mark ended their EXPLORE process with, "Brenda, this feels good, and thanks for coming forward with your insights."

Mark could have chosen to hear only the complimentary part of Brenda's comment. Or, if he focused on the constructive criticism part, Brenda might have felt put on the spot. However, seeing that the information could be valuable, he chose to use STOP–HELP–ASK and RISK to EXPLORE and learn more. Great opportunities can come along at any time—often not at the most convenient time. Brenda's remark presented an opportunity. How we handle opportu-nities like this can make all the difference.

EXPLORE Tip: Acknowledgment Is Important

As EXPLORE unfolds, some ideas will be left behind and some may change dramatically. This natural process of selection and creativity allows everyone to reach success.

That doesn't mean that ideas left behind aren't valuable. They may have been the catalysts needed to move to the next levels. Everyone's participation is essential to make EXPLORE work. Acknowledgment fosters participation.

Acknowledgment comes in two different forms:

1. Acknowledgment and reinforcement of ideas, concepts, information, considerations, or whatever else is flowing through the conversation; and

2. Appreciation: letting others know how grateful we are for their involvement and support.

Both are important. Along the way, don't forget to give yourself some silent "way-to-go's" as well!

Some examples of acknowledgment in the conversations between Noal and Mark and Noal and Lou include:

- Mark accepting and appreciating Noal's input about the EXPLORE examples.

- A general acknowledgment by both that Noal's observation "we're having an EXPLORE conversation right now" is a major aid in moving things forward.

- Mark summarizing what needs to be done, and in so doing acknowledging and memorializing the process and the results.

- Noal acknowledging her and Lou's previous success and helping make sure that success is continued.

- Both Noal and Lou acknowledging how important the conversation is.

- Lou owning his challenges with touchy-feely conversations, which opens doors that might have stayed closed for months.

In the Marvin/Rick/Pam example:

- Marvin avoids focusing on blame and uses STOP–

HELP—ASK to find out what's happening and how he and others could be involved.

• Marvin coaches Rick and Pam to EXPLORE, helping Rick and Pam codevelop their solutions, knowing that he needs to let them work things out themselves.

• By advancing additional ideas about how the teams might work together, Marvin makes it acceptable to RISK and opens the door for Rick and Pam to do the same, without going to a "my idea/your idea" mind-set.

• He stays involved long enough to ensure that this interaction will be successful.

There is power in simple words of praise such as the following, but feel free to use your own words:

• "Thank you."

• "Interesting idea."

• "I appreciate your contribution."

• "Please tell us more."

• "Can we expand that?"

The more specific you can be with praise and acknowledgment, the better:

• "Thank you for suggesting the reorganization of the warehouse."

• "Thanks for following up on the customer data we discussed. It made all the difference."

EXPLORE Tip: Easy Does It! Don't Forget STOP-HELP-ASK

EXPLORE can be fast-paced, so it's important to support EXPLORE with the other Tools; otherwise, you may miss out on real benefits. We worked with a client who had two dynamic executives: the Chief Operating Officer (COO) and the Director of Human Resources (HR). They both used the Tools effectively, but between their forceful personalities and strong friendship, they often leapt into RISK and EXPLORE without first taking full advantage of STOP-HELP-ASK, and they sometimes lost track of where they were headed with their insights and possibilities.

A while back, they met to create an employee survey that both thought would be valuable for organizational effectiveness. Each had previous experience with surveys, but they hadn't done one together. Their conversation quickly moved to EXPLORE as they threw survey ideas back and forth: questions to include, when they'd send it out, and how they'd analyze results. They had a great time and immediately implemented their plan.

Unfortunately, they hadn't spent time talking through the broader goals, issues, and implications of the survey, including any unintended consequences. Because they didn't lay the groundwork with STOP-HELP-ASK up front to clarify intended outcomes, consider the current organizational climate, anticipate the survey's impact on the organization, figure out how to get department heads' buy-in on completing the survey, and discuss how they might utilize the survey results (would this be a confidential survey, and who would see the results?), the survey created turmoil and opposition in the organization. As a result, the entire process required more time and energy than might have been necessary if they'd slowed down and used STOP-HELP-ASK in the planning stages.

In Noal and Mark's conversation, when Noal shifts gears to discuss the manuscript schedule, Mark does a STOP–HELP–ASK to make sure he knows where she's going with the new subject.

In Noal and Lou's conversation, Noal does an internal STOP, realizing that she can't let her first stalled phone conversation with Lou get in the way of success. She uses ASK for clarification about what happened in that conversation, and for permission to advance the conversation.

In Marvin, Rick, and Pam's conversation, Marvin uses STOP to prevent himself from overpowering the meeting, not saying: "I'm the boss and you will do it my way." He uses STOP–HELP–ASK to clarify what is being presented and to ensure that everyone is still on the same page, and he uses collaborative questions to bring the three of them together.

If you aren't sure exactly what to ASK, you might say something that acknowledges the value of everyone's participation and also slows things down a bit: "This is exciting and I'm tempted to plunge ahead, but let's just STOP a minute and ASK whether we've covered all the bases. Are there some issues or considerations we might be missing?"

EXPLORE Tip: Use ASK to Encourage Participation and Action

It's not always easy to get everyone to participate. Some may be hesitant to join in when everything is moving quickly. Sometimes the conversation gets hijacked by more expressive personalities. ASK can open doors to let everyone into the conversation.

- **"I'm wondering how XYZ might work, and I welcome feedback from each of you."**

- **"If we try ABC, how would that affect your department?"**

- "I like this time line, but I'm not sure how it might work with our budget for next year. What should we request from accounting?"

- "How might we work with each other to move this idea forward?"

- "Is there anything we haven't considered that we should be considering?"

New ideas and information can come from anywhere and anyone. Sometimes we don't understand how important our contributions can be and need encouragement to open up.

EXPLORE Tip: Prepare to Be Surprised!

Once everyone is interacting, you may be surprised at the energy and excitement EXPLORE creates. That's good! Energy and excitement allow people to open up to even more creative ideas.

RISK alone creates a lot of energy: "This may sound crazy, but I am going to RISK here. I've been thinking that, if we could move shipping and receiving to the back warehouse, we could resolve a number of distribution challenges, clean up our frontage, look more presentable, and acquire more space for production. Is this a good time to discuss this?" A big idea such as this could open a flood of other big ideas. With an honest RISK and a receptive audience, the conversation that follows could be animated and profitable.

So, leave preconceived ideas behind when you go into EXPLORE. Be open to new concepts and perspectives. ASK open-ended and collaborative questions like:

- "If we increase our marketing efforts, where do you think I should put my energy?"

- "If we terminate Jack what must you consider for your department?"

- "What can I do to support you and this situation?"

- "What questions can we ask that will help shift our thoughts?"

- "In what areas can we get the most information?

- "What are the risks and the benefits?"

EXPLORE Tip: Take Time—Slow Down

If you know you want a conversation that will include EXPLORE, plan ahead so that you'll have enough time. Not only does it put people at ease to have time to EXPLORE, but you mitigate the disadvantages of finding out later that you missed something that could cost a bundle to fix, or you lost an opportunity for additional profits, increased market share, an enhanced image, or other benefits.

If EXPLORE happens spontaneously and there's not enough time at that moment, set aside time in the near future to continue. You might say, "Marcie, this is great. We're really getting somewhere, but I've got to meet with Steve. When are you available to get together again so we can continue to EXPLORE?" Be sure to set the date and time. To keep the energy going and stay on the same page, highlight the next meeting's agenda points and prioritize them.

EXPLORE Tip: Set Up More EXPLORE

If during EXPLORE it becomes clear that a final resolution won't be reached in one sitting, it's important to reach a decision on interim steps toward a successful result. Doing this demonstrates that people have made a positive difference and affirms that they're working on something important that won't be dropped once the meeting is over. Most of us will invest energy when we know that our energy will be put to use. Here are some examples of ways to use ASK for this purpose:

- "In what areas should we be researching our options?"

- "What can we do to be ready for a meeting on Tuesday?"

- "Should we invite the accounting department to join our next discussion? What will they need in order to be prepared?"

- "How comfortable are we with option X?"

- "What do we need to do to begin developing action steps?"

- "What feedback do we need from others before we can proceed?"

For complex projects or issues, EXPLORE can be used multiple times in multiple sessions to move forward. Just set up interim steps as "bridges" to your next EXPLORE session. Here are some examples:

- Interviewing for a job. You don't have the job yet, which is the final resolution. Through the interview process, you can learn about the business and the prospective employer learns about you. Next steps in EXPLORE may include ASKing about scheduling follow-up interviews within the company, and continuing your broader job search.

- Identifying a new product or service. Through EXPLORE, you may determine that you need to add a new product or service. Reaching this decision is an important initial step. As you EXPLORE opportunities for selling the product or service, you may create action plans that involve more research or development. You have moved the project forward, though you are still evaluating the process and the "go or no-go" of this new service or product.

• Agreeing to merge with or acquire a business. Having discussions and exploring the implications of buying or merging businesses can be a lengthy process. Once it's been decided that this concept has merit, you've advanced the process, but there is much to be done before you can complete the transaction.

• Agreeing on final candidates for a job. Selecting the final candidates has moved you closer to filling the position. Though the task is not complete, you are moving toward resolution and now need to identify what has been accomplished and what still needs to addressed.

• Planning a conference. Finalizing the location is a time-consuming and important decision, and EXPLORE can help you come up with options, narrow them down, and make a selection. Then EXPLORE can continue to help you formulate action steps for arranging the conference at that location.

EXPLORE Tip: Reduce Resistance by Making Sure Everyone's on the Same Page

Debbie, the marketing director for a client that uses the Tools, told us about a meeting she had with Ed, vice president for business development. "I had an idea for a new service area that I had researched. I arranged a meeting with Ed to discuss it. I'd worked with Ed for a while and we'd used the Tools often. I thought this would be an easy discussion.

"I set the stage with STOP–HELP–ASK. It was easy to go to RISK because we got on the same page quickly. When we entered EXPLORE, Ed liked the idea. After we talked for a few minutes, though, he got so wound up with how we should market it that I couldn't get a word in. I tried STOP, but Ed kept going. He had gone in a direction that didn't fit the service area, and he was invested in his idea. When I did get him to STOP to ASK a question and try a course correction, he paused—then went back to his idea!

"I don't think Ed intended to steamroll me. He got caught up in his view of this potential service area and the more he talked, the more invested he became. I must confess, I did give up and decided to approach it again another day.

"In our next meeting, we got the new service idea on the table. I realized that I hadn't used STOP on myself enough and was not open to what Ed was saying. Using STOP–HELP–ASK, I was able to get myself back into the conversation and we both moved into EXPLORE. We reached a decision that we should develop this new area and Ed and I became jointly responsible for the project."

Had Debbie not been so skilled with the Tools, Ed's well-intentioned zeal might have cut her out of the collaboration and caused her to lose enthusiasm. We could appreciate Debbie's dilemma. Ed is a powerful force when he gets going. Debbie has expertise in the service area, yet Ed didn't seem open to her contribution. Ed needed a stronger reminder that he needed to keep the conversation open so that Debbie could contribute her experience, too. We talked to him later and he told us he thought her idea was so great that he got too excited thinking of possibilities, never realizing he had overwhelmed the situation. It was a strong reminder that EXPLORE works better when everyone is actively engaged. STOP–HELP–ASK helps ensure that everyone is included.

Later on, Debbie, resilient as ever, was able to talk to Ed and discuss what happened. She realized she had always been on the team in Ed's eyes. When they launched their plan, she received a substantial amount of credit for their innovations.

EXPLORE Tip: Staying on Track

EXPLORE can feel chaotic and confusing, so it's important to be aware of circumstances that can impede or slow down the process along the way:

- Quiet people can get lost in the excitement and may not participate fully.

- It's easy to go off on tangents if we forget where we were headed in the first place—for instance, remembering the RISK that started it all.

- Subconversations can get started within the group. You may need to bring everyone back to the main conversation, while at the same time acknowledging the importance of what had them huddling together in discussion.

STOP–HELP–ASK are there for you at these times. For example:

- To clarify an idea: "Pete, can I ASK you a quick question? When you say we should use an outside service, are you thinking short term or longer term?"

- To understand: "Ned, I'm confused about our outsourcing customer service and need HELP. What are some of the benefits for our customers?"

- To engage participation: "Barry, you have great ideas, and I'm wondering how they will affect client interaction and our client service. What do you think, Sarah?"

- To prevent your steamrolling: "I'm sorry, Jen, I seem to be moving a bit too fast. I know you want to say something. In what ways have I reinforced or contradicted what you are trying to say?"

- To keep everyone on track: "Great ideas, but I'm confused how these fit into or could be blended into our older product lines. Am I missing something?"

- To build on an idea: "This is a powerful approach. I'm curious: how does it relate to our original conversation? What comes to mind?"

- To regroup when people are no longer on the same page: "Ned, I'm unclear about what you're saying about Chuck's idea. Could you could HELP by discussing your thoughts in more detail?"

S.H.A.R.E.™ Tools in Action

How EXPLORE Transformed and Saved a Business

We were consulted by a large manufacturing operation facing business failure. With many years of success behind them, they were suddenly confronted with a "perfect storm" of events that threatened to sink them, including eroding customer loyalty, an unsupportive bank relationship, operational challenges caused by a new IT capability, and liquidation. Chaos was the best description for this once-pristine, efficient environment. The bank viewed the situation as desperate. Vendors were clamoring for money. Nonoperating shareholders were investigating legal options. The employees, preoccupied by stress and fear, were not performing well. And customers were becoming disgruntled by slow service.

Resolving this complex situation required all the players to bring their best game. The S.H.A.R.E.™ Tools helped us restart, reinvigorate, or improve lackluster or eroding interactions and get everyone moving in the same direction. In particular we worked with the bank to establish a dialogue so they could get a better picture of what was happening and could see that things weren't quite as hopeless as they thought. A reporting and interactive process was set up that the bank could rely on for current and accurate information. After each meeting with the stakeholders, the bank, shareholders, and other professionals, progress reports were created that highlighted successes and the continual efforts being made to resolve the situation—thus getting as many people on the same page as possible.

On the customer service front, the company had moved to a voice mail–driven ordering system, but it turned out that customers missed—you guessed it—conversation with a live human being about their orders and any problems. The voice mail–based ordering system was downplayed and a receptionist-like system was reinstituted to ensure that customers' calls were answered by people, not computers. We helped the staff with S.H.A.R.E™ Tools–based dialogues so they could better help their customers. To prevent order delays, a procedure was initiated in which all order desk personnel, armed with the ordering histories of regular customers, would call assigned customers to ask whether they might wish to place advance orders, expressing the company's desire to make sure that the order was promptly processed and delivered on time. So, rather than wait for the customer's call, the company reached for HELP and RISKed by anticipating what the customer's next order might look like.

Many of the employees were interviewed individually and were asked to share their concerns and perspectives, engaging them in the process. We were then able to reach out to the staff with helpful information about how things were changing while also thanking them for their support.

Finally, we held a three-day corporate meeting that brought together team members from across the company. They became the stars, describing their situations, ideas, challenges, and successes. Using EXPLORE again and again, they created the vision for how the company could adopt more effective methods and be even better than it was before. This was the first time the managers and supervisors had been in the same place at the same time. It was powerful for all of us to be in that room and watch them passionately seize the opportunity to contribute to the saving of the business.

Results: Shipping returned to normal. Customer support improved. A new credit line was created, and a much better working relationship was forged between the bank and the company. Profitability returned to normal. Sales increased. And all of this was done in record time.

Everyone worked long hours, but together, through a persistent commitment to collaborate, support each others' ideas, and EXPLORE solutions, everyone was open to examining what would work and how fast it could happen. Thanks to the employees' dedication, this company was saved and became more successful than before. In fact, once they saw how well their ideas were working, they continued to generate more ideas and improvements. In this way, the Tools seed the habits of better interactions, increased support for the ideas of others, and the ability to seize opportunity, anticipate and solve problems, manage disasters, and enhance success whenever possible.

EXPLORE Chapter Key Concepts

- EXPLORE is a high-energy place to be.

- Downshifting to STOP–HELP–ASK can repeatedly refresh conversations and clarify ideas and concepts along the way.

- RISK allows new ideas to emerge and creates an atmosphere of collaboration so that everyone participates.

- EXPLORE advances the process, creating goals and benchmarks to define measurable action steps.

Adding Value with EXPLORE

- Creating something new that contributes to a business being more successful.

- Bringing people together to use their collective knowledge to solve problems and improve situations.

- Developing a stronger team through the shared creative process.

Action Steps

Powerful change happens in EXPLORE, but you'll need all the S.H.A.R.E.™ Tools to make it work.

- It is essential to be open to what RISK makes available.

- When taking a RISK and moving into EXPLORE, remember to bring along STOP–HELP–ASK for clarification and understanding.

- When discussing options in EXPLORE, ensure that everyone understands and is on the same page.

- In meetings, be sure everyone participates so that the group can reach the best, most viable resolutions.

Your Observations

- What changed at work now that you are using EXPLORE? At home?

- What value did you add today with EXPLORE?

- What did you learn when you used EXPLORE to solve problems?

Our Observations

EXPLORE is a productive place to be. It stimulates a creative atmosphere that develops tangible, meaningful solutions and resolutions that weren't possible before. Remember that EXPLORE is only as good as the possibilities that are created and offered in RISK and developed through STOP–HELP–ASK. A colleague shared this experience:

"I had been working with several clients in the same industry on a project. Certain aspects of it just weren't working. As I talked with other industry contacts, I learned information that could be valuable to the project. I started to put the pieces together and came up with an entirely new way to bring these clients together. When I called the point person for the project and reviewed the information, I expected him to reach the same conclusion. I was talking with him as if my new idea was already in place. When he began to push back with questions, I realized that we weren't ready for EXPLORE. I hadn't built a foundation with him for what this new information meant to the project. Fortunately, I was able to pick up on the problem and go back to STOP–HELP–ASK, then RISK putting the new idea forward, so we could EXPLORE it together. Once we did that, the pieces came together for him, too, and we moved ahead."

His story reminded us how easy it is to get caught up in the momentum of EXPLORE, and how using the S.H.A.R.E.™ Tools internally can be just as important as using them in conversation.

CHAPTER 7

CREATE YOUR OWN REVOLUTIONARY CONVERSATIONS™ WITH THE S.H.A.R.E.™ TOOLS

You can enjoy the benefits of Revolutionary Conversations™ by using the five proven S.H.A.R.E.™ Tools. They are easy to remember, and the more you use them, the more skillfully you will achieve your goals. We believe you'll notice positive differences in your life as you embrace them in your conversations.

They work best if you can remember and implement the foundational aspects noted in chapter 1:

- Coming alongside others to avoid "my idea/your idea."

- Seeking to find out "what happened?" and not "who's to blame?"

- Focusing on success by relying not on what we know, but on what we need to know.

- Avoiding "telling" and focusing on a collaborative/contributory approach with others.

- Acknowledging your own and others' contributions along the way.

> • Letting others clearly understand and appreciate that
> you want to collaborate and engage.

Even without the Tools, these philosophical approaches can work wonders in increasing your ability to be more productive and more successful. What the Tools are exceptional at is helping you manifest these approaches in real time, and in real-life situations. They are extraordinary at helping to eliminate confusion, conflict, embarrassment, and failure.

There are many ways to remember and use the Tools. Some students place a "S.H.A.R.E." note on their telephone or notepad to remind them to use STOP, HELP, ASK, RISK, and EXPLORE. You don't have to be perfect or spend hours preparing or practicing. The S.H.A.R.E.™ Tools are forgiving and can be effective even if you're new to the process. Each time you use them, you're opening the door to using them better next time.

The shift starts with you. But as you change your conversations, you'll find that others change their perspectives about conversations, too.

Letting Go

There are a number of philosophical practices and learned behaviors that you may need to let go of in order to feel most comfortable and most effective in using the S.H.A.R.E.™ Tools. The most common are the following:

> • Learning that it's OK to STOP someone who is talking
> in order to find out more—as long as you're not trying to
> take the conversation away from that person. In this case,
> the constructive interruption of STOP is a positive action,
> not a social faux pas. Many of us have been trained to

never interrupt. We wonder what the consequences of that edict have been over the generations . . . what do you think?

• Becoming comfortable with the idea that getting HELP is brave, resourceful, and smart. Not reaching for assistance even in the smallest of ways can result in wasted time, lost opportunity, embarrassing mistakes, and most of all the disappointment of letting others down. HELP is a lifesaver.

• Embracing the idea of not trying to convince others you are right. As we've said, it's not what you know that will make you successful, but what you need to know. Assuming that you know (and thus are right) leaves out all other good ideas, energy, and resources that others can contribute to make any situation better. And it's really not good PR to be seen as a know-it-all.

• ASKing questions from a broader, more collaborative perspective. We've all heard that we need to ask good questions. But when asking questions verges on or even has a whiff of being an interrogation—as in looking for the culprit—collaboration quickly exits stage left! Using ASK to understand and to help others understand can take some getting used to when many of us have become accustomed to searching for errors as opposed to looking for opportunities.

• Taking time to prepare for what you're going to say. If you feel that what you have to say is important, it's a worthwhile effort to advance it when it's most appropriate. We have many students who admit that before learning the Tools, they led with RISK in most interactions. They were out there letting everyone know their insights, ideas, concepts, impressions, feelings, and more. What they have come to learn is that RISK before STOP–HELP–ASK is like fire, ready, aim and usually has the same result: a missed opportunity, an embarrassing moment, or worse.

• Realizing that there's more to conversation than talking and listening. There is interaction—the space between, around, and over talking and listening. This is where the S.H.A.R.E.™ Tools shine by bringing together all of the factors, influences, information, and individuals involved to make talking and listening much more dimensional, and a whole new experience.

As with any change process, it will take time and a bit of effort to come alongside the Tools and become comfortable with letting go of previous habits and impressions of how conversations work. Please give yourself time to acquire the skills and to become comfortable with the whole process.

Putting It All Together

Not all interactions are conversations or dialogues. Many of our exchanges are simple declarative interactions: "Please get/find/look up/order/ask about this"; "Here is the report"; "I'd like two burgers, fries, and a Coke"; or telling the taxi driver where you need to go. But the Tools can come in handy during any interaction, even if all they do is to slow you down a bit so that you're actually saying what you mean, hearing what you need to do, and being heard by others.

As you work with the Tools, you'll find unique ways to use them. You'll discover many things about yourself and others as you find ways to add value to every aspect of your life. Here are a few thoughts to consider:

• The S.H.A.R.E.™ Tools create a structure for Revolutionary Conversations™ by moving conversations forward in a productive, respectful way.

- Anyone can use the S.H.A.R.E.™ Tools, regardless of education, communication style, or position in an organization.

- Using the S.H.A.R.E.™ Tools can get work done faster, more easily, and more effectively.

- When people are having a Revolutionary Conversation™, a unique synergy of language and energy is created that increases the value of their communication significantly.

- The S.H.A.R.E.™ Tools can deepen relationships with business associates, family, and friends because the Tools ensure that we understand each other and create a space where everyone can contribute.

- The mind-set behind the S.H.A.R.E.™ Tools is inclusion, not exclusion, as they tap into the resources of everyone involved.

- The more you practice the S.H.A.R.E.™ Tools, the better they work.

- As others experience you using the S.H.A.R.E.™ Tools, they feel a comfort level that allows them to come alongside and use the Tools instinctually to make conversations better.

- Regardless of the circumstances, the S.H.A.R.E.™ Tools are always there to support you and your conversation partners in contributing and adding value.

How to Start

Starting off can be a challenge, but it can also be a pleasure. There's nothing in the Tools that you haven't done before. Of course you've stopped someone; you've asked for help; you've asked a million questions; you've risked reaching out with an idea, not knowing what was going to happen; and you and everybody around you have all explored new ideas.

What's different about the S.H.A.R.E.™ Tools is that they give you a language and a framework for doing these things in a more organized, engaging, and productive way. They are exceptional resources that will make a difference in your daily life, especially if you can embrace the foundational aspects above.

One of the best ways to start is to talk with someone about this book and what you've learned and see how they react. Who knows, it might start a whole new way for you to converse with this person!

Taking a S.H.A.R.E.® Workshop is obviously another way to advance what you've learned. Another way is to start a book club where you can read and discuss material with a group of like-minded friends and/or associates.

Another very effective way is to expand your conversation with a friend about the Tools into a collaboration to get better and better at using them after you've both read the book or taken a S.H.A.R.E.® Workshop. In the appendix, you'll find material about S.H.A.R.E.™ Pals, which was created by Barbara as a way to help her and a friend solidify and grow from what they both learned in one of our workshops—It has stuck and they are still conversing weekly after three years.

But the great thing about the Tools is that you can use them right away. So why not just start?

We think you'll find that most people will respect your need to find out more, and rarely do people push away a request for help. When others feel respected and heard, it adds harmony in a world where conversations can be combative, contentious, unproductive, or hurtful. The S.H.A.R.E.™ Tools and principles make it possible to turn conversations around. Every successful conversation has the potential to diminish anger, fear, resentment, and frustration and instead foster acceptance, understanding, acknowledgment, and resolution.

One of the biggest challenges to using the Tools is simply remembering to use them. The three of us often find ourselves in the quagmire of realizing that we missed a great opportunity to use the Tools—it usually happens fifteen minutes after leaving the meeting or interaction. What we've had to learn is that we can't be perfect. We have to be satisfied and reward ourselves when we use the Tools and learn from the times when we don't. (Sometimes we find that the Tools help us reopen the conversation: "You know, I was thinking about our conversation/meeting/phone call, and I realized I could really use some HELP. . . .")

Lifelong Learning

Even after a quarter of a century of developing, refining, and teaching the Tools, we discovered many new features about them as we developed this book. We find that we learn more about the S.H.A.R.E.™ Tools in every conversation with every person. Each time we think we've heard all the ways the Tools can be used, we experience or learn of another conversation where the breakthroughs delight us. Every interaction becomes an opportunity to discover more about others and to add value and richness to our lives. In this way, the S.H.A.R.E.™ Tools support lifelong learning—personal, professional, intellectual, emotional, and more—that can enhance not only competitiveness and employability, but also social inclusion and personal development.

Remember that the Tools do not work against what you already know; they assist you in expanding your existing skills and knowledge. And you can start working with any of the Tools just by tapping into the conversations that are happening right in front of you—there's no need to wait for the "perfect" opening. Remember, too, that the Tools are forgiving: you can make mistakes with them and still benefit and learn. For instance, if you realize that you tend to plunge straight into RISK and then find yourself playing catch-up because people need to come alongside, that insight in itself is huge. You can then learn to STOP yourself internally and manage RISK to reduce unnecessary work and stress and have more effective and productive conversations—a great reward!

The Tools do not have to dominate how you perform your work or live your life. They're simply there to assist in situations whenever you need them. If you accessed the Tools just twice a day, you could focus on those moments, increase the efficiency of those conversations, and enhance the clarity of your interactions and quality of those relationships—worthy goals, for sure. Enriching a single conversation a day with the S.H.A.R.E.™ Tools will reward you exponentially.

Now, It's Your Turn

The Tools were born out of a desire to accelerate and maximize outcomes of our work with our clients. We wanted to leverage our input and enhance results by having everyone more involved and committed to change. People are the essential force for making change happen, not just at work, but everywhere in our world. The Tools harness that powerful force.

The S.H.A.R.E.™ Tools have been credited with saving many businesses. They are a proven asset, time and time again, in business and life in general.

As you use the Tools, you, too, can create advantages for your world. Don't leave home without them. Take the S.H.A.R.E.™ Tools with you wherever you go. Experience them. Build stronger, more dynamic relationships with everyone you know—and reach out to those you don't know. Watch your relationships change and improve . . . your career grow . . . your business prosper. With the S.H.A.R.E.™ Tools, you have the power to create Revolutionary Conversations™ that solve problems, launch ideas, build stronger relationships, and navigate the challenges of life with grace and strength. We wish you the greatest success!

Let's keep the conversation going!

Collaboration produces amazing results. It did for us, and when you try it, please let us know how it worked for you. We hope you will contact us by e-mail at: info@revolutionaryconversations.net.

To order additional copies of *Revolutionary Conversations*™ or to learn about our trainings or workshops, please visit our website:

http://www.revolutionaryconversations.net/ or call: 805-968-8567

To contact us by regular mail, please write to:

Revolutionary Conversations, LLC
P.O. Box 2028
Santa Monica, CA 90406

S.H.A.R.E.™ Pals: A Way to Practice Having Revolutionary Conversations™

S.H.A.R.E.™ Pals is a partnering relationship that lets two or more people support each other with updates on how they're using and experiencing the Tools. Barbara has maintained a S.H.A.R.E.™ Pals relationship with a member of one of our S.H.A.R.E.® Workshops—it was an idea that emerged from the workshop, and Barbara and her Pal both felt it would help them retain the Tools and practice them in a safe environment. We know Pals who practice using the Tools in conversations with family members. One Pal had an important breakthrough with a son. In some of those conversations, the Pal would become so frustrated that the Pal would say, "That's it, I'm done!" Finally, the Pal did a STOP to get some HELP and asked, "Can you HELP me understand what's going on?" Ultimately, the Tools supported their conversations and significantly contributed to their understanding each other, which helped both parent and son move toward a positive relationship.

We hope you'll give S.H.A.R.E.™ Pals a try. This book can be your operating manual for reference and review.

How to Pal

You can make your S.H.A.R.E.™ Pals updates as formal or as informal and as private or as public as you like. You can update each other by e-mail, phone, in person, or via online video. You could start a discussion group online. If you're into social media, you could even post your thoughts about using the S.H.A.R.E.™ Tools on your blog or on other social platforms and create a big, open community.

How often you connect with your Pal(s) is up to you and them. A friend and her Pal have talked to each other on the phone every Saturday morning since participating in the S.H.A.R.E.® Workshop. It can be useful to touch base weekly, especially at first, when you're getting the hang of both the Tools and the Pals process.

The Intention of S.H.A.R.E.™ Pals

The intention to keep in mind when using Pals is that you are supporting each other in learning and navigating the S.H.A.R.E.™ Tools through discussions about:

- What was learned and experienced when using the Tools?

- What needs to be learned about using the Tools?

- Daily awareness about using the Tools in conversations and interactions

Helpful Tips

- Structure helps. Set aside time to have conversations with your S.H.A.R.E.™ Pal and commit to using the Tools.

- Pals may choose to exchange e-mails with each other a few times to be sure each is committed to becoming a Pal. You will learn about your similarities and differences as you get to know each other and discover whether this is the right Pal for you. You may need to ask: Will we be able to continue as S.H.A.R.E.™ Pals? If not, there may be another Pal out there for you.

- Even if you already know your potential Pal, it's a good idea to make sure you both have the same intentions about using and helping each other with the Tools. Take the example of our friend. Although she and her Pal already knew each other, in order to come alongside as S.H.A.R.E.™ Pals, they reintroduced themselves and talked a little about how they'd like to make use of the Tools, which included discussing their lives, their families, their work, what their days are like, and similar topics.

A Sample S.H.A.R.E.™ Pals Schedule

The sample five-week schedule below is just that—a sample you can use to get started, elaborate on, or use as a jumping-off point for creating your own customized schedule and themes for discussion with your Pal.

Week 1

Theme: The S.H.A.R.E.™ Tools are forgiving.

Introduce yourselves as you come alongside each other to become S.H.A.R.E.™ Pals. You can learn more about your Pal with his/her permission to look at websites and blogs, too. Talk about yourselves and your daily lives, sharing whatever feels comfortable.

- How did conversations and interactions go last week?

- Did you have conversations or interactions that were important or that you would like to discuss?

- Have you had opportunities to use all or any of the Tools in your conversations?

Commitment: Set day/time for weekly conversations to discuss the Tools.

Homework: At least two conversations using the Tools during the coming week.

Week 2:

Theme: How are the S.H.A.R.E.™ Tools working for you? Be alert to good opportunities to use the Tools.

Talk about how the Tools worked during the previous week, including:

- How did you feel about your conversations last week? Describe a conversation and its benefits.

- In what situations were you able (or not able) to use the Tools? What helped you remember to use the Tools?

- When using the Tools, how did they help conversations flow?

- Consideration for Journaling: Sometimes Pals use journaling to document their experiences as they use the Tools.

Homework: At least two conversations using the Tools during the coming week.

Week 3:

Theme: Enjoy each conversation as a gift. Pay attention to what presents itself to you in each conversation.

Reflect and review how the Tools worked during the previous week:

- Are your partners in conversation paying attention and/or involved in conversations?
- Discuss the importance of remembering to use the Tools as often as possible and focus on which techniques help in remembering to use the Tools.

Homework: At least two conversations with the Tools during the following week, including with family, plus journal at least twice.

Week 4:

Theme: The S.H.A.R.E.™ Tools work with those near and dear, especially family.

- Reflect and review how the Tools worked during the previous week:
- Which family members did you feel most comfortable engaging with, and why?
- Which areas of those discussions were the most important for using the Tools?
- Do you see ways that the Tools could be helpful in conversations at/about school, work, home, chores, family events, or budgets?
- Did you try journaling? If so, how did the experience of journaling affect your use of the Tools?

Homework: At least two conversations with the Tools during the following week plus journal at least twice.

Week 5:

Theme: Conversations with the S.H.A.R.E.™ Tools make life more wonderful for us and the people we connect with . . .

Reflect and review how the Tools worked during the previous week:

- In what ways did knowledge of the Tools improve?

- What breakthroughs were most important?

Homework:

- More conversations using the Tools during the coming weeks

- Journal more

- Think about some specific changes you would like to make and how the Tools might help you get there. One group of Pals got so excited about the Tools' power that they decided to look at where they wanted to be in five years and used their journals to reflect on the transformations they were currently experiencing in their lives, and on their goals.

The rest is up to you. Help each other discover the value of the S.H.A.R.E.™ Tools in each conversation. Have fun!

ACKNOWLEDGMENTS

This book is the result of the collaboration and participation of the many people we've worked with, talked with, laughed with, and loved. Please know you are appreciated and we acknowledge your invaluable support. Thank you all for learning along with us and helping us practice the S.H.A.R.E.™ Tools.

As we mention and repeat often in the book, collaboration, "power with," a team approach, and seeking the moments of success help make projects like this truly successful. We would also like to give special thanks to the following people:

Toni Sciarra Poynter, our editor extraordinaire, who provided insight, clarity, friendship, great laughs, and just the right words to bring the S.H.A.R.E.™ Tools to life in this book.

Our friend Charlotte, who asked one day out of the blue, "Where is that book?" and then proceeded to keep us moving forward, capturing every word of our vibrant conversations and helping us build the foundation of our story.

Colette Laurent, who added the S.H.A.R.E.™ Tools as one of her many languages and who has supported us and helped us find deeper meaning in the process.

Paul D. Supnik has been with us from the start. He has kindly watched over us making sure we understand, appreciate, and honor the integrity of our creations. He is always there making sure we are on target.

Lou Esbin, who pushed us to think differently and brought us new perspectives on the dimensions of the Tools.

Dr. Robert Muller, who showed us the power of creating peace by using the right words to achieve an honest connection with every person we meet.

Jim McDonald, who read the very first version and the last, gave us his keen analytical insight, and helped us find gems of wisdom hiding in plain sight.

The readers who eagerly beta-tested the manuscript and provided extraordinary value through their thoughtful comments, clear focus, constructive feedback, and probing questions.

The people who have attended our workshops and who supercharged our learning by adding vibrancy and energy to every aspect of the S.H.A.R.E.™ Tools.

The team at the Ambrose Hotel in Santa Monica who helped in so many ways to create an exceptional environment every time for our workshops and brainstorming conferences.

Every aspect of this journey has been a team effort, and we would jointly like to acknowledge each other. We have had an amazing team learning experience, and each one of us has contributed at each step in the conceptualization and writing of this book. The critical framing of ideas happened as we stayed in touch and made sure everyone was on the same page. We knew that the others were watching our backs and we appreciate how much time, energy, emotional sweat, and intent everyone has put into this cherished project. We are a team and are so appreciative that we wrote this together.

Mark H. Fowler
President, Stowe Management Corporation
(www.revolutionaryconversations.net)

Mark H. Fowler specializes in transitioning companies from challenge to achievement with a focus on enhancing revenues and profits. For more than twenty-five years, he has assisted businesses in moving from symptom through problem to resolution, resulting in expanded distribution networks, technological developments, new products and services, improved profitability, increased corporate value, and enhanced corporate image. Using his knowledge and experience in corporate development, expansion programs, and business turnarounds, Mr. Fowler has assisted hundreds of businesses with corporate reengineering. His expertise includes growth management, strategic direction, business plan implementation, capability analysis, cash and financial management, systems integration, corporate reorganization, and merger and acquisition placement. His close working relationships with clients have resulted in his assuming such positions as vice chairman, chief operating officer, chief financial officer, and administrative officer.

Mr. Fowler is a member of the American Institute of Certified Public Accountants (AICPA) and the California Society of Certified Public Accountants, serving as Committee Member/Chair/Speaker and presenting at more than forty California CPA Education Foundation conferences. He has written numerous articles, created more than twenty-five courses, and has presented more than fifty different speeches to professional organizations on topics such as corporate expansion, crisis management, management for success, marketing strategies, effective communication for greater success, and management consulting.

Noal McDonald, MAOM, SPHR

Noal McDonald is a seasoned professional in human resources and operational management. She is currently the chief operations officer for a CPA firm in Encino, California. In this role she is responsible for managing all aspects of the firm, including HR, marketing, technology, training and development, recruiting, and facilities.

Working internally with organizations and through her own consulting firm, she has helped companies make significant cultural changes by designing and implementing HR departments, creating staff and leadership training programs, developing comprehensive talent management processes to attract and retain top candidates, and instituting policies and procedures that ensure legal compliance. Industries she has worked with include professional services, not-for-profit, media, manufacturing, and retail. She holds a master's degree in organizational management, is certified through the Society for Human Resources Management (SHRM) as Senior Professional in Human Resources, and is a member of the American Society for Training & Development (ASTD).

Barbara Gaughen-Muller

Founder of Gaughen (GONE) Global Public Relations in Santa Barbara, California, Barbara Gaughen-Muller has devoted her life to a better world and serves as president of the Santa Barbara and Tri-County chapter of the United Nations Association of the United States of America (UNA-USA). Inspired by her late husband, Dr. Robert Muller, former United Nations Assistant Secretary-General (www.RobertMuller.org), and her mentor Edward Bernays, her socially responsible public relations firm is now in its twenty-fifth year. Previously she was the director of the Industry Education Council and the National Alliance of Business.

Her public relations company has won numerous awards, including Best PR Firm for five consecutive years. Current clients include Bragg Live Food Products, Inc. and Patricia Bragg, Dan Poynter, Global Ebook Awards (www.globalebookawards.com), and National Urban Search and Rescue. Author of *Book Blitz*, she created National Book Blitz Month, held annually in January, to honor the world's authors, and she is past president of the Book Publicists of Southern California. Her radio show, *Inspiring Conversations,* featured business, educational, and spiritual leaders and was broadcast worldwide from the Radio for Peace International. Together with Robert Muller, she developed daily E-ideas for a better world, which can be found at http://www.goodmorningworld.org. She was a Hollywood Rotarian, is a Creative Member of the Club of Budapest, and serves on the board of Surgical Eye Expeditions (SEE) International.

NOTES